POPULAR ART DECO

POPULAR ART DECO

DEPRESSION ERA STYLE *and* DESIGN

ROBERT HEIDE *and* JOHN GILMAN

ABBEVILLE PRESS · PUBLISHERS

NEW YORK · LONDON

Editor: Walton Rawls
Designer: Molly Shields
Copy Chief: Robin James
Production Manager: Dana Cole

First paperback edition

10 9 8 7 6 5 4 3 2 1

Library of Congress Cataloging-in-Publication Data
Heide , Robert, 1939–
      Popular Art Deco: depression era style and design/ Robert Heide and John Gilman.
          p. cm.
      Includes index.
      ISBN 0-7892-0823-7
      1. Art Deco—United States   2. Art, Modern—20th Century—United States   I.Gilman, John, 1941— .II. Title
N6512.5.A7H45 1991   90–48164
709'.73'09041—dc20   CIP

Jacket illustrations (top to bottom, left to right):
Encharma cold cream complexion powder box, Luxor Ltd., Paris, Chicago, New York; La Bouquet talcum powder, Jay's Chemical Corporation, Brooklyn, New York, Lithograph on tin, ca. 1932; license plate attachment, enamel on metal, featuring the famous Mobil Oil red Pegasus created for Socony-Vacuum Oil Corporation by Jim Nash in 1937; Florida Deco Flamingo playing cards, made in U.S.A.; streamlined Sunbeam Mixmaster with green "Jadite" glass bowl, c. 1932; hand-painted ceramic pitcher showing "streamlines" and a stylized fish, made in Japan, ca. 1930s; aerodynamic, streamlined-moderne, "teardrop"-style Cyart table-model radio, made of molded red Plexon and trimmed with clear Lucite, 1946 model; tango Orange glazed-ceramic vase in combination skyscraper-sunburst-fountain Deco style; Depression green frosted-glass cigarette box supported by 1920's flappers of painted green iron. Title page: Chromium "Turnover" toaster featuring an Art Deco fountain motif. Westinghouse Electric Manufacturing Company. Mansfield Works, Mansfield, Ohio, ca. 1927. Frontispiece: Catalin radio display (top to bottom): first row Emerson "Cathedral," 1937 and 1938; second row; Motorola, 1941; third row: Fada, 1940 and 1941; fourth row: General Electric, 1941; fifth row: Sentinel, 1945.

This new edition of Popular Art Deco is dedicated to the memory of Barbara Baer Capitman, Jeffrey Geiger, Tim Goetz and John Rothermel

Acknowledgements

From the New York Art Deco Society: Kathryn Hausman, Glen Leiner, Harriet Selzer, Bob Josen

Robert Abrams, Louise Kurtz, Laura Tepper, Josh Abrams, Molly Shields, Walton Rawls

Dianne Pilgrim, Sanford Smith, Irene Stella, Joan Tramontano, William H. Straus, Laurie Gordon, Mary Goldie, Nena Chavarria, Wendy Lipkind, Madeline Hoffer, Louisa McCune, Philip Cohen, Seth Joseph Weine, George Bouras, Stephen Hooper aka 'Hoop', Mel and Eunice Birnkrant, Helen Harrison, Joyce Johnson, Michellle Kelly, Kenneth Anger, Joe Franklin, Peter Gilman, Jeffrey Painter, Sean Boyd, Robert Bryan, Jon Glick, Sara Baysinger, Lita Solis Cohen, Linda Jonasch Artalie, Nancy Keller, Jeremiah Newton, Peter Mintun, David Sheward, Bill Prensky, Jim Fitzgerald, Jonathan Walsh, Joseph Lanza, Noam Dworman, Andrew Shand, M. Jennifer ex Bowen

Ted Hake of Hakes Americana and Collectibles, Rich Conaty of Radio WFUV, Michael Smith of Depression Modern, Michael Riedel of the New York Post, Lynn Yaeger of the Village Voice

The Cooper Hewitt, National Design Museum

Photo Credits

Principal photography by John Gilman.
Additional photography by Suzanne Fitzgerald Wallis (pages 197, 198, 199); Philip Cohen (pages 189, 192); Tim Goetz (pages 30, 43, 86, 193, 204 upper right); John Kardies (pages 190 upper right, 191); Robert Kuebler (page 33 bottom).

Permission from Barbra Baer Capitman, Miami Design Preservation League (pages 45 and 208)

Opposite: *Seeing the New York World's Fair* by Elsie Jean, an officially licensed children's activity book, McLoughlin Bros., Inc. Springfield, Massachusetts, 1939.

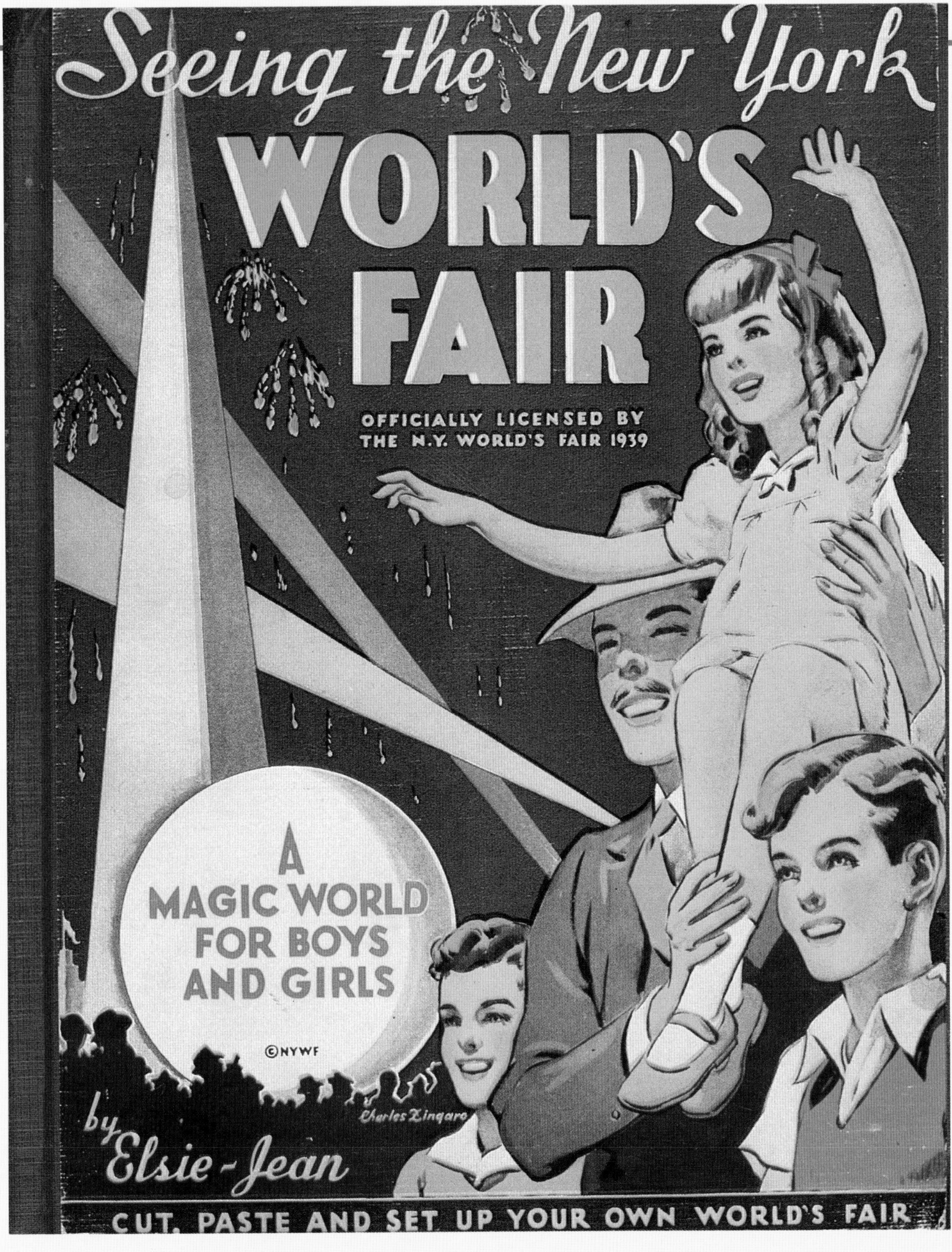
Seeing the New York
WORLD'S
FAIR
OFFICIALLY LICENSED BY
THE N.Y. WORLD'S FAIR 1939
A
MAGIC WORLD
FOR BOYS
AND GIRLS
©NYWF
Charles Zingaro
by
Elsie-Jean
CUT, PASTE AND SET UP YOUR OWN WORLD'S FAIR

CONTENTS

Keep on the Sunny Side of Life

A new way of living

DECO COMES OF AGE

In recent years the term *Art Deco* has come to include a much broader range of objects, graphics, and furnishings than when it first caught America's attention in the 1920s and '30s and then again in the 1960s. Early modernist mass-produced artifacts that not too long ago were regarded as "kitsch" are now examined from a new perspective and with greater appreciation. Consequently, many of these items have moved into higher-priced categories in the "new antique" marketplace. In the 1980s, to differentiate Depression-era mass-produced Art Deco–influenced artifacts from original, limited-production French and European Art Deco of the 1920s, dealers, collectors, and writers began to use the catchall phrase *popular Art Deco*. For the purposes of this book, the term is meant to encompass those popular modern and streamlined items designed and manufactured for the millions of consumers eager to embrace the "world of tomorrow" as a way of dealing with the Great Depression: the kind of forward-looking objects and design graphics that people lived with every day in the late 1920s and '30s.

In surveying the wide variety of affordable products bearing the imprint of Art Deco—whether actually sold in dime stores or not—it seemed almost obligatory in this volume to extend the category of the mass-produced into the realm of radios, appliances, furniture, architectural decoration, and transportation, where the influence of this design style was clearly pervasive. Even though the average middle-class American (who considered himself lucky to have any kind of income) could not easily afford a blue-mirror and chromium Sparton radio or drive a Chrysler Airflow or dance in the Rainbow Room or travel regularly aboard the new streamlined trains, he certainly aspired someday to partake of such luxuries—as so many popular songs in the Depression made it clear: "Keep Your Sunny Side Up" and "Make Way for Kid Prosperity."

Mass marketing and mass production, as they are

An American family of the 1930s with their pet Scottie dog on the cover of a health-diet recipe pamphlet published by W. K. Kellogg, Battle Creek, Michigan, 1933.

known today, came directly out of early explorations of the machine aesthetic of the 1930s and the new concept of merging art and industry. Much of what was produced is surprisingly effective and sophisticated by today's standards. It is as if the machines used in modern manufacturing processes were in competition with fine craftsmen of earlier times to produce quality that now could be achieved by using technology. These early mass-consumer items leave us with a rich heritage of unique objects that are very striking and important in terms of what we collect and use today as "Deco."

The architecture critic of the *New York Times*, Paul Goldberger, noted in an Art Deco Society newsletter in 1982 that a broad-range concept of Art Deco was then beginning to take hold, but this was not necessarily seen as conflicting or competing with strict constructivist viewpoints held at the inception of the movement. In fact, much of Art Deco has always included a cross-current of modernist styles, for some of it was created for a high-priced market and some for mass consumption.

In the early 1930s, a gentleman "painting the town red" at an Art Deco–style nightclub might have lit his lady's cigarette with either a flash-zip Deco-designed Ronson lighter or a paper matchbook with strong Deco advertising graphics on its cover. By the same token, though milady's cigarettes may have been kept in a Deco-style smoking case, the original cigarette package would also have been designed in a modernistic style, be it Lucky Strike Green, Spud, Wings, or Fatima.

The top commercial artists of that period (in retrospect now regarded as first-rate artists in their own right) not only designed consumer-goods packaging and advertisements but book-jacket graphics and even matchbook covers. In similar fashion, influential indus-

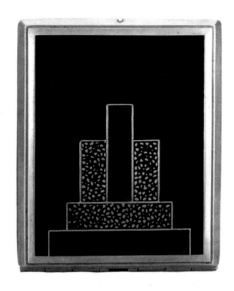

trial designers continuously helped create new products in the 1930s for an ever-growing marketplace. Lionel Tiger, professor of anthropology at Rutgers University, pointed out in a *New York Times* article in January 1987, that "Our things help define who we are. Old things confirm that we have perdured, we have come through. They are easier to appreciate if

Cigarette case, chrome metal and green enamel, Evans Manufacturing, 1930s.

Presto cigarette case, metal and black lacquer with pseudo-eggshell and skyscraper motif.

Engraved gold-leaf leather card and note case, August Sirk Co.

Roy Lichtenstein's Modern Painting with Bolt, *1967, oil and magna on canvas; collection Sidney Janis, New York, gift to Museum of Modern Art. Photograph by Rudolph Burckhardt.*

Commemorative bronze medal, A Century of Progress, Chicago, 1933.

NRA Member, "We Do Our Part," National Recovery Act store-display statue, painted metal alloy.

the art cognoscenti announce that they are beautiful." Tiger also noted that the old objects, and not just those that have reached official antique status, were always well designed and constructed. *They* have remained the same. *We* have changed. He claimed that industrial designers are really the folk artists of our civilization and that the work they did, *objets* from a relatively recent past, are as vital and reflective of our life and times as the ceremonial treasures we line up on museum walls.

Under the same influence that Art Deco had had on the style and imagination of the 1920s, artisans who designed objects in the 1930s invested their furniture, architecture, and utilitarian artifacts with a sleeker, more modernistic style that was pleasing to the eye and easier to live with. It is this spirit of a forward-looking "over-the-rainbow" optimism in the midst of a great Depression that we are dealing with in this volume. As Little Orphan Annie told her dog, Sandy, in a comic strip from the early 1930s, while she happily cooked up a Depression meal on the stove, "If you work hard enough even in—hard times—you can find that chicken in a pot on your very own stove!" Americans who were not on relief or standing in breadlines struggled and toiled through the Great Depression, and to motivate and inspire them, architects, designers, and manufacturers produced an unending panoply of new buildings, products, and designs that were uniquely American. At the New York World's Fair of 1939–40, visitors were eager to view the World of Tomorrow, which promised, among other things, that someday gas and electricity would cost them just pennies a year. This fair, which was a tribute to the ideas of the modernist movement, became the stylistic zenith of the 1930s, which now may easily be referred to as "the design decade."

In the late 1980s, Deco came to be regarded as a "classic" twentieth-century style, with two important museum shows focusing just on Art Deco in America. "The Machine Age in America, 1918–1941" originated at the Brooklyn Museum and traveled to Pittsburgh, Los Angeles, and Atlanta, and the Smithsonian Institution's National Museum of American Art's "American Art Deco" was launched at the Renwick Gallery in Washington, D.C., and traveled to Miami, Omaha, Tulsa, and St. Paul, Minnesota.

Some of the prime Deco design examples culled from popular culture that are now prized and cultivated as "mainstream" Deco by connoisseurs of this style are presented and interpreted here. Although yesterday's dime store Deco has not overtaken the original French-manner Deco or examples of designer Streamline Moderne, the two extremities of Art Deco do regularly complement each other at popular antique shows or in auction-house catalogs.

Little Orphan Annie ceramic Ovaltine mug, radio premium from the Wander Company, Chicago, Illinois, 1933.

Little Orphan Annie "plug-in" Depression-green enamel on metal toy stove with electric coils for children to heat up their pot of Ovaltine, 1933.

DECO ORIGINS

The term *Art Deco* is derived from the name of the 1925 Paris Exposition Internationale des Arts Décoratifs et Industriels Modernes. This mid-1920s world's fair of innovative decorative arts and architecture is generally acknowledged as the starting point from which neoteric styles of design began to take firm hold in both the European and American marketplace. In the late 1920s and early 1930s, the advanced concepts developed at the 1925 exposition were most often referred to as simply "modern" or "modernism." Other descriptive terms used during those early years were Art Moderne, Jazz Moderne, and the New York Style, the latter referring to the city's craze for higher and higher skyscrapers.

It was only in 1966 when the Paris Musée des Arts Décoratifs held its retrospective of design styles emanating from the 1925 exposition that the catchall expression Art Deco began to come into popular usage in describing the revival of interest in that form. In the aftermath of intense focus in the late sixties and early seventies, Art Deco was often shortened to a quick, convenient "Deco," e.g., a Deco vase, Deco jewelry, or a Deco building. Thus we also began to hear mention of "the Deco style" in painting, graphics, objects, and furniture.

In reality there were rumblings of what came to be known as Art Deco, or modernism, even prior to 1925. In 1908 the new dress designs of couturier Paul Poiret were presented by Paul Iribe in book form in Modigliani-like drawings of elongated fantasy women in billowing garb that now look Art Deco. In 1912 Poiret opened a design studio in Paris, Atelier Martine, where he sold his attractively packaged Deco-style vials of perfume in an atmosphere of modernity reflecting advanced German and Austrian design. There was also the important influence of Sergei Diaghilev's Ballets Russes dance company, which came to Paris in 1909 with abstract geometric forms in patterns for costumes and stage-set motifs. The Munich Werkbund, whose motto and purpose was to create a union

White-metal figural mood-lamp with green bronze finish on marble base by Max LeVerrier, height 20". Available originally from LeVerrier's prominent Paris design art studio, ca. 1925.

between art and industry, including crafts and architecture, first established workshops in 1907. Although France had originally planned to have a modernist exhibition on public view by 1915, the advent of World War I postponed this exposition until after the war. René Guillère, founder of the Société des Artistes-Décorateurs, had opened the shop Primavera in Paris prior to World War I, but it was not really in full operation until after the war when its workshops were implemented.

The Bauhaus also had a strong impact on modernism in the early 1920s. Founded in Weimar by Walter Gropius in 1919, the Bauhaus collective moved to its newly designed, starkly modern headquarters in 1925. There, the influential group created bold new technics and models for industry and housing, espousing sparse decorative schemes for their interiors. Chief director of the school until 1928, Gropius eventually emigrated to the United States where he became chairman of the Graduate School of Design at Harvard. Until the Bauhaus was closed down in 1933 by the Nazis, men like Richard Neutra, Hannes Meyer, and Ludwig Mies van der Rohe continued to pursue their aesthetic of

French Art Deco table clock in blue terra-cotta, ca. 1925.

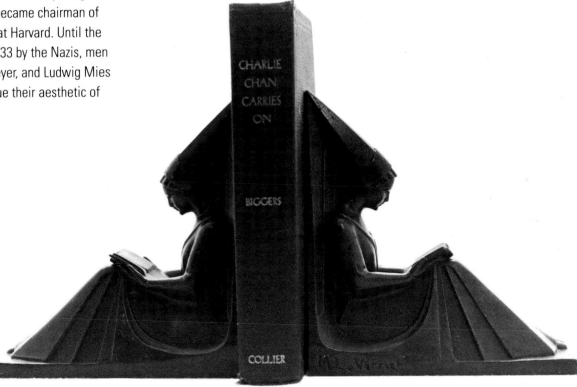

White metal bookends with a green-bronze patina depict storybook Rennaissance-style women reinterpreted in the Art Deco mode. Signed M. L. Verrier, the pair was sold at Primavera, Paris, 1925.

Glazed-ceramic vase with zigzag motif, Germany, late 1920s.

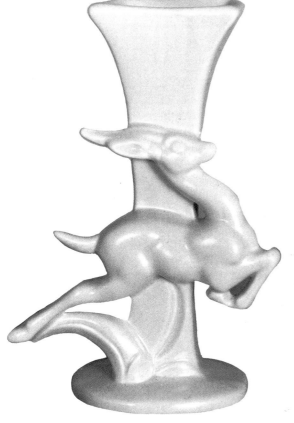

Glazed-ceramic bud vase with leaping deer, ca. 1930s.

Asia magazine, January 1929, painting of Oriental dancer in feather headdress by Frank McIntosh.

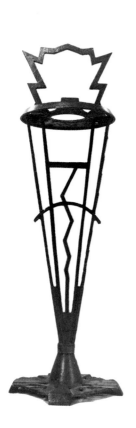

Mantel windup clock of French metal on marble base with electric lights behind yellow celluloid featuring two Casino de Paris show-girl nudes, with zigzag, floral, and sunburst Deco motifs, signed Limousin, 1925.

''Les Fontaines,'' 10½ in., souvenir plate made in England for the 1925 Paris Exposition Internationale des Arts Décoratifs et Industriels Modernes.

Lightning-bolt standing ashtray, height 27 in., made of iron and painted green and orange. Made in the U.S.A., 1920s.

the purely linear and functional, which came to influence one very important aspect of Art Deco. Curiously, while Hitler had a distaste for modernism, his black swastika symbol set against a white circle upon a red background is pure Bauhaus. Among others, American Indians had used the swastika, weaving it into their tapestries and baskets. While some of the Bauhaus design ethic is traceable to American Indian tribes that employed variations of the purely geometric in everyday utilitarian objects such as blankets, rugs, teepee coverings, ceramic jugs and bowls, garments, and jewelry, as well as their imaginative decorative arts, much of the strict and formal modernism of Bauhaus had its roots in the aesthetic of the machine.

The Bauhaus dictum was to aid in the evolution of the technology of the machine and mass production. The prefabricated units employed in advanced housing estates exhibited at Weissenhof in Stuttgart in 1927 were examples of this. The Bauhaus as well as the Dutch De Stijl movement were excluded from the 1925 Paris exposition because they expressed little regard for French ornamentation, preferring to focus on the linear and geometric aspects of modernity. Many "ism" movements also proved to be important in the development of Art Deco as a formal design style, including Dadaism, whose exponents equated men with machines even though they were opposed to mass production; Surrealism, which was meant to reveal the subconscious as influenced by the industrial complex; Cubism and Fauvism, which were characterized by geometric components of images and bright and violent colors; and Vorticism, Futurism, Constructivism, the Wiener Werkstätte of Vienna, and the Munich Werkbund, all of which emphasized machines in their manifestoes.

French Art Deco initially incorporated the rectilinear and functional applications of the Bauhaus, but, in conjunction with this, added on elements of exotic curvilinear motifs adapted from Art Nouveau. Large baskets of zinnias or cabbage roses or cascading fountain motifs were applied right alongside stronger geometric patterns. The opening of Tutankhamen's tomb in 1922 helped to create an interest in reinterpretations of Egyptian scarabs, pyramids, sphinxes, coiling snakes, elongated cats, and ziggurat progressions—themes that often occur and reoccur in Art Deco design. Aztec and Mayan cultures exerted their influence as old civilizations with monumental temples and the bright hot colors of sun and desert. Decorative motifs from Assyria and Byzantium are also to be found in this modern format. African tribal designs and subject matter, including Zulu masks, jungle cockatoos, giant tropical leaf patterns, and other symbols coming out of primitive cultures were also integrated into the overall original concept of Art Deco.

"Double-bud" vase featuring satyr on one side, nymph on the other, silver glaze on ceramic, marked Primavera, 1925.

DECO INVADES AMERICA

American buyers and designers from department stores and in the fashion, graphics, and print industries went to the 1925 Paris exposition in search of new ideas that could be mass-marketed in the United States. The exposition included examples of modern architecture, innovative fashion and fabric design, and interior decoration and furniture design contributed by Italy, Russia, Poland, the Netherlands, Austria, Sweden, Denmark, Japan, Monaco, Czechoslovakia, Belgium, Spain, and Great Britain. France, of course, gave the exhibition its main thrust, incorporating in its exhibits all of the modern motifs in design and crafts developed in Europe since the beginning of the twentieth century. The modern grandeur of this exposition instigated a design revolution in America. Americans had earlier been oblivious to modern commercial design concepts, so when Secretary of Commerce Herbert Hoover was invited to contribute to the Paris exposition he declined, stating that America had nothing to offer that might be construed as being "modernistic." German modern movements were noticeably absent.

American architects and designers brought back from Paris not only the concept of merging art with industry, which was just what they had been looking for, but also a bold new modern design style that could be applied to architecture and to items designed to be manufactured on a mass scale. The bold geometry of this style included an overlay of romantic French-manner influences that featured elongated nude nymphets, leaping gazelles, tiered water fountains, lightning bolts, vivid sunburst patterns, and intricate floral and fern arrangements. Images showing a fascination with acceleration and speed in action, such as airplanes, automobiles, or women dancing in "moderne" masklike faces with hair flying out behind them in zigzag progression, were some of the dramatic and appealing design elements that came into play in early Art Deco.

Modern zigzag table lamp designed by Donald Deskey, 1927–31. Often sold in pairs through specialty design shops and in department stores, the lamp is nickel-plated metal with glass. Deskey-Vollmer, Inc.

When Deco finally arrived in America after 1925, it was fully embraced by the sophisticated connoisseur, city dweller, jazz-baby flapper, and the elite cognoscenti. It was, however, regarded with suspicion by wealthy and pious industrialists who along with the greater middle class had come out of old-fashioned or immigrant backgrounds that did not easily welcome change or the idea of "modern liberation." Nevertheless, no one could escape the fact that something new and challenging was in the air.

Part of this modern transformation was that women who once played their roles only in the home were now becoming active participants in the work force. With the burgeoning of the machine and industrial-complex economy, women were being employed in offices as secretaries, typists, and telephone operators. Others not seeking glamorous careers in theater or motion pictures were sometimes working as waitresses or bartenders or even as speakeasy hostesses, like the famed Texas Guinan who shouted out "Hello, suckers!" to the throngs of businessmen who entertained clients and girlfriends in her New York nightclub. New employment opportunities, along with 1920s fashions that called for above-the-knee short skirts, brought forth a more independent woman who now defiantly smoked Lucky Strike or Camel cigarettes in public, danced the Charleston all night long in jazz clubs, and drank bathtub gin with the gusto of any man. Modernity as a life-style was beginning to take hold in America.

Another major thrust into American culture for the modern or Deco movement was packaging design and commercial products geared toward mass-market consumers. Perfume bottles, rouge and powder boxes, soapboxes, coffee tins, ink containers, and cigarette packaging all had to appeal to the idea of a modern new world that was to be dominated by technology

Judge *magazine, September 25, 1926, showing the modern blonde flapper that gentlemen preferred in the 1920s.*

Modern Youth, *February 1933, cover design by Philip McGuire.*

and the machine, promising a future dream of a perfect civilization geared to the comfort and pleasure of the masses. However, many people feared this new machine aesthetic, feeling that machine domination could ultimately destroy the human race. Books written and illustrated by John and Ruth Vassos, who created manifestolike tomes such as *Contempo*, *Humanities*, *Phobia*, and *Ultimo*, expressed a concern about the machine and the kind of fascist conformist society it might help to create. The idea that the individual might be swallowed up into the whole of the machine complex was expressed by Stuart Chase in *Men and Machines* (1929) who projected the "evil effects" of the future as:

Too many machines; excess plant capacity;
Riotous waste of natural resources;
Too much labour in distribution and the overhead services;
Unemployment, cyclical and technological;
A badly balanced flood of goods, often useless, often adulterated;
Super-congestion in urban areas;
A devastating ugliness in many regions;
Smoke, noise and dust in needless volume;
Over-mechanized play.

Echoing other sentiments concerning the role played by the machine was C. A. Glasgold in an essay entitled "Design in America" from the book *American Design* (1930):

We see ourselves immersed in a mechanical civilization and we fear lest the values of life be submerged beneath the inhuman weight of the machine. In some, this fear has tended to provoke a vigorous condemnation of the machine age and to arouse a

nostalgic, yet vain longing for "the good old days." Nevertheless we must accept contemporary conditions. It is utterly impossible to undo what has already been accomplished by Taut, Le Corbusier, Van der Rohe, Wright, Gropius and others. Besides, and what is more important, by the exercise of intelligence we can force the machine into the service of beauty.

This conflict of fear and acceptance was also depicted in Fritz Lang's powerful 1926 German silent film *Metropolis*, which showed the exploitation of the worker who toiled at machines dominated by the wealthy capitalist bosses who partied constantly in their vast, sumptuous Art Deco skyscraper office suites.

Perhaps the realization that mankind could be reduced to cowering slaves in the march of industrialization prompted the U.S. Supreme Court in 1926 to uphold the constitutionality of local zoning in New York that set the stage for the future development of high-rise buildings. Strict height and setback controls were imposed on skyscrapers, ensuring light and air at street level so that cities would not become a network of dark canyons.

Jumbo Bakelite pen and original box, ca. 1930s.

Modern packaging design: Waterman's Aztec brown ink bottle, ca. 1930. Carter's Kongo Black ink, ca. 1930.

Mohair fabric in a russet-colored circular pattern with three streamlines set against a pearl-gray background, used as a "tidy cover" for a standing Victrola, ca. 1928.

American-made console table designed by G. Siegrist and executed by the Sterling Bronze Co., New York City, used nickel and chromium plate on bronze with exposed bronze chevrons, ca. 1934. Atop the table is a white metal mantel clock with matching lamps featuring celluloid inserts, two Casino de Paris show-girl nudes, signed Limousin, 1925. Made in France, this windup clock with electric lights was sold at the famous Primavera shop in Paris.

Brushed chromium-plated metal and glass clock designed by Gilbert Rohde, manufactured by the Herman Miller Clock Co., Zeeland, Michigan, 1933.

In the final analysis, Americans embraced the idea of the machine as a tool of progress. A sense of futurism, optimism, and indomitable confidence persisted in industry and in modern design, even in the decade that was to follow the stock market crash of 1929. The Depression decade of the 1930s saw a new aspect of Deco design emerging in the marketplace: Streamlining. The streamlining concept created by industrial designers, some of whom had formerly worked as set designers, architects, or interior decorators, stripped Deco-design of its fauna and flora in favor of the aerodynamic-pure-line concept of motion and speed culled from scientific thinking.

An array of designers in the 1930s like Paul Frankl, Walter von Nessen, Raymond Loewy, Norman Bel Geddes, Gilbert Rohde, Donald Deskey, and Russel Wright ultramodernized and streamlined the designs of everyday things, focusing primarily on their function in a new marketplace. Manufacturers of clocks, lighting fixtures, radios, telephones, radiators, ships, trains, cars, buses, trucks, furniture, vacuum cleaners, mixers, and other common household appliances competed annually with dynamic new models making their appearance in stores and showrooms each January—an eagerly awaited event.

Beauty parlors, corner soda fountains and candy

shops, shoe stores, dress shoppes, offices, diners, restaurants, bakeries, and nightclubs were all enthusiastic about gaining more business through modernizing their premises in the new industrial materials of chromium steel, colored, marbleized, or black Vitrolite glass, tubular neon, clear glass brick, tinted mirrors, and recessed lighting. Americans who were not on the dole or standing in breadlines and could afford to make a purchase or use a service flocked to these sleek, shiny emporiums of modernity.

The varying interrelated modernistic styles that contributed to what we now espouse as American Art Deco did not entirely cause a divorce from the 1925 French-manner ornamentation style. On the contrary, the French Deco movement was also incorporated into the mass marketing of many objects. However, the chief momentum of the day became "less is more." American contributions like streamlining or the skyscraper motif ultimately came to dominate the 1930s, in that these were tailored specifically to the demands of industry. Today, the multifaceted machine-made artifacts, many developed by first-rate American industrial designers from the age of early modernity, are at the very heart of the American Deco experience. This does not lessen the importance or the impact of the original French craftsmen or artisans whose fine renderings now command high prices at galleries and auction houses and are collected by museums around the world. It does demonstrate how Americans reinterpreted even that form to suit their own commercially oriented needs.

In America, a fast-paced modernity took a particularly strong hold not just on the world of packaging and products, or on decorative objects and furnishings, but on advertising promotion as well—in advertisements, matchbook graphics, magazine covers, and book-jacket design. Terms such as *Modernism, Art*

Moderne, Streamline Moderne, Industrial Moderne, Jazz Moderne abounded in the 1930s, but today we tend to think of all of these as belonging under the umbrella of Art Deco, or just Deco. In writing on the style of the 1920s and '30s we have used each of the above terms in different categories to apply to a specific situation or design concept. This only points to the signs along the road that led to the overall use of Art Deco to cover these numerous interrelated styles.

The way in which modernity and Art Deco entered every phase and aspect of American life and the extreme popularity of the concept of modernization became a uniquely American experience that was, at first, considered highbrow, but eventually became the nonelitist property of everyone. In the middle of the Great Depression, it seemed that everybody began to adopt the idea of "going modern," either in their present circumstances or at some future time when they could afford it. The idea of a Future Moderne was there in almost every new product in the Depression; or it struck you each time you entered a redesigned super-Deco modernistic Automat restaurant or a neonized stainless-steel streamlined diner. By the 1930s the machine aesthetic, the merging of art and industry, had implemented itself into American culture.

Historically Art Deco came to a stop as a style following the New York World's Fair of 1939–40. The World War II years seemed to demand a more squared-off look for everything, almost as part of the defense buildup against the enemy. Greta Garbo left M-G-M, and America imported a more subdued and robust Greer Garson in her place. In the aftermath of the war, with servicemen returning from years of deprivation and women toughened by working the swing shift in defense plants, the materialistic fifties decade came into full stride. Though some of the new scarab shapes in postwar automotive design, such as the Hudson, Lincoln, Mercury, and Nash, resembled the cars of tomorrow shown in the Futurama exhibit at the 1939 World's Fair, it was ultimately the rocketship shape for cars and the flying saucer and boomerang shapes that dominated the fifties aesthetic. Art Deco remained as if asleep and forgotten until the mid-1960s revival. Author Thomas Hine states in his book *Populuxe* (1986) that "America went on its greatest shopping spree from 1954 to 1964, buying a vast array of new gadgets to fill up their split level Levittown suburban homes." Following that surfeiture, the trend back to Deco came into play.

DECO REVIVAL

"With justice, so far, we can describe Art Deco as the last of the total styles."—Bevis Hillier, 1967

The popular revival of Art Deco that began in 1966 with a retrospective exhibit at the Paris Museum of Decorative Arts brought together the work of European designers who participated in the 1925 exposition.

A year later, in 1967, the movie *Bonnie and Clyde* was released. Based on exploits of the notorious Barrow gang, the picture depicted the bizarre relationship between Bonnie Parker and Clyde Barrow, who robbed banks in the Midwest during the Great Depression. At first a "sleeper," this period-set film eventually caught on as an underground hit with the sixties counterculture and subsequently with the general public. A virile, handsome Warren Beatty in a pinstripe suit, felt hat, and bold-patterned silk tie and sexy young blonde newcomer Faye Dunaway in sixties versions of thirties fashions created somewhat glam-

orous portrayals of what life "on the lam" was all about. The picture also seemed to reflect the deep unrest and anger of the late sixties; and it almost augured a later situation in which a rebellious Patty Hearst found herself, like the legendary Bonnie, inside a bank armed with a machine gun.

Establishing robbers of the Depression era as almost mythic folk heroes and Robin Hood rogues doomed to die at the hands of the G-men, the 1970s and '80s American Deco movies that followed were akin to such original flicks made in the 1930s such as Public Enemy with James Cagney and Jean Harlow or Little Caesar with Edward G. Robinson. The newer films also sparked a keener interest in the 1920s and '30s and a desire to view the vintage classics, particularly on VCRs, over and over again. *Bonnie and Clyde* was the first of a series of big technicolor movies in which the vintage cars, clothing, location, settings, and props caused as much of a sensation as the actors and the story.

The Chrysler Building is the quintessential Art Deco skyscraper, embodying the emblazonment of automotive progress. Designed by architect William Van Alen for Walter Chrysler, it was completed in 1930. The main entranceway at 405 Lexington Avenue and two other entranceways on 42nd and 43rd streets lead into a most fantastic, pyramid-shaped red marble Art Deco lobby with dim, mysterious coved cold-cathode lighting.

This is still the case in recent films (*The Godfather, Godfather II, Godfather III, The Last Tycoon, Brighton Beach Memoirs, Purple Rose of Cairo, Chinatown, Radio Days,* and countless others) wherein the background details, the props and costumes, and particularly the restored classic automobiles receive a great deal of onscreen attention from film producers and directors. This trend toward meticulous Deco reproduction achieved high-art status in films like *Chariots of Fire* and the television series *Brideshead Revisited.*

In one film sequence in *Bonnie and Clyde*, the criminal couple find themselves hiding out in the balcony of a dingy movie theater like the ones depicted in the paintings of Edward Hopper. We see Faye Dunaway as Bonnie watching an onscreen Ginger Rogers (wearing an outfit made of oversize silver coins) singing with a chorus of platinum blondes, "We're in the Money," from Busby Berkeley's *Gold Diggers of 1933*. Early zany black-and-white musicals that are replete with Art Deco sets, props, furnishings, costumes, and detail began to turn up with great regularity at revival houses and museum film retrospectives, attracting crowds of new audiences who had never seen them originally. The late-late shows on television that previously aired these pictures, considering them outdated relics for insomniac TV viewers, soon could no longer easily obtain the rights to show them. Apparently distributors began to withhold "forgotten" films, realizing that more money eventually could be made by creating a new marketplace for them. All of this occurred, of course, well before the advent of videotape sales and rentals.

Concurrent with the *Bonnie and Clyde* phenomenon, which opened up a wellspring of powerful nostalgia for the decades to follow, was the reemergence of Walt Disney's *Fantasia* as a hit with the freaked-out drug-acid subculture. This almost psychedelic film,

Official "Bonnie and Clyde" song folio (featuring on the cover, left to right, actors Gene Hackman, Estelle Parsons, Warren Beatty, Faye Dunaway, and Michael J. Pollard) was published in 1967 by M. Witmark & Sons. Inside are photo stills from the movie and the songs "Bonnie and Clyde" with words and music by Charles Strouse, "Sometimes I'm Happy" with words by Irving Caesar and music by Vincent Youmans, and Al Dubin and Harry Warren's "The Gold Diggers' Song—We're in the Money" and "The Shadow Waltz."

with abstract images and cartoon characters set against a classical soundtrack conducted by Leopold Stokowski, was a highbrow flop in its initial release in 1940. Decades later *Fantasia* became an embarrassment to the Disney Studio when it was clear that its major attraction to new young audiences in rerelease was that the film served as a visual counterpoint to getting high. Many young viewers in the sixties swallowed sugar cubes soaked in LSD to "get into" the fantasy and technicolor animation swirls of *Fantasia*. The obsession with *Fantasia* was reported as a new phenomenon by *Life* magazine, and the film is still shown to new audiences who contribute to the redolent odor of marijuana always in the air. Many of *Fantasia*'s configurations, like the sequence featuring the goddess Artemis, depicted with bow and arrow shooting at the night sky, the dancing Chinese mushroom people, the pterodactyls, unicorns, centaurs, centaurettes, and mythic gods and demons, had a specific visual link to Art Deco. The Disney artists who worked on the film had, of course, been directly influenced by the Art Deco movement of the 1920s and '30s.

In searching thrift stores, flea markets, and garage sales in the late sixties and early seventies for items specifically from the thirties, young hippies, rock stars, and connoisseur collectors suddenly began sporting authentic 1933 Mickey Mouse or Big Bad Wolf wrist-watches, wearing bright yellow, green, red, and or-ange 1930s Catalin jewelry, carrying original period compacts with ziggurat design motifs, and decorating their apartments with the three-piece overstuffed

maroon mohair furniture sets and blue-mirrored cof-fee tables just recently thrown out of attics or given away by their parents to the Salvation Army. In fact, many Art Deco treasures in the late sixties were rediscovered at secondhand emporiums like the Sal-vation Army, St. Vincent de Paul, the Goodwill, or in junk and thrift shops. The sales people at such places generally regarded this "old merchandise" as junk, and certainly never heard of Deco. Designer chrome furniture of the 1930s was regularly discarded on the street or could be bought at junkyards for scrap-metal prices.

The sixties "tune in, turn on, drop out" message was purported to be connected to the opening up of a new spiritual age. Referred to in the musical *Hair* as "The

Deco-patterned man's tie, 1930s.

Miami Beach Art Deco Week celebration and Antique Auto Show on Ocean Drive, show-ing the Tides and the Victor hotels, 1986.

"Dawning of the Age of Aquarius," the visual input, epitomized with popular commercial Deco graphic interpretations by artist Peter Max, went hand in hand with the Art Deco revival. Max even painted the exterior of a renowned Swami's private jet plane in the Pop-Deco style of the sixties. One could see the original brilliant themes of the early movement in the graphics for rock concert posters, which used Day-Glo colors but, nevertheless, owed a debt to Art Deco. Pop artist Roy Lichtenstein literally mirrored the Deco images and forms in the 1960s, incorporating them into his paintings and metal sculpture. The continuation of the machine aesthetic as an integral part of the development of Art Deco is often seen in the work of other Pop artists like Claes Oldenburg and Tom Wesselmann. The latter included yellow and red 1930s Streamline Moderne radios into his oversize airbrush paintings. Andy Warhol echoed the machine aesthetic by repetition of the Campbell's Soup can or Brillo box in the manner of assembly-line mass production. Warhol, in fact, became one of the chief exponents of original Art Deco, amassing a huge top-notch collection of furniture, jewelry, glassware, chandeliers, statuary, and other related period objects. Other celebrity

connoisseurs of the Real-McCoy Deco are Barbra Streisand, who began collecting when she portrayed Fanny Brice in *Funny Girl* on Broadway, John Lennon and Yoko Ono, who furnished their apartment at the Dakota with authentic Frankart painted-green-nudie and fanciful-fun Art Deco statuary, ashtrays, and mood lamps; and Mick Jagger, who was often seen at the auction houses bidding on finer Deco items. The cover of one of Paul McCartney's *Wings* record albums is a photograph of a Chiparus Deco bronze-and-ivory statue of a thirties showgirl in an Erté-like "winged bat" outfit. Singer-actress Bette Midler haunted Manhattan's famous 26th Street outdoor flea market on Sundays in search of *chotchkes* and schlock from the 1920s and '30s. An outrageous acting troupe called The Angels of Light dressed up in exaggerated glitter costumes and sang happy Depression songs like "Keep Your Sunny Side Up!" in cabarets in San

A 1930s home-hobby collage in a wood frame used a magazine cutout of a dancing Mickey Mouse and a background of jazzy Deco-patterned wallpaper.

Streamlined overstuffed club chair in rose mohair, ca. 1937. (Collection of Second Hand Rose, New York)

Francisco and New York. Deco always seemed to appeal to show-business cognoscenti; George Gershwin and Noel Coward and many others decorated their ritzy apartments in the 1930s in Art Moderne.

In 1968 a book by English art historian Bevis Hillier called *Art Deco* was published in a small paperback format at $2.95, with illustrations on quality paper stock of elegant Deco objects primarily from the French school and from Great Britain. This was the first book to employ the term Art Deco in examining the modern styles of the twenties and thirties, and it became the handbook and guide for studies to follow. Collectors and auction houses avidly began to seek out French Art Deco, often discovering pieces in import-export trade shops at extremely reasonable prices, or in grimy secondhand shops on the Bowery where they were being sold as junk, scrap metal, or as kitschy, outmoded decoratives. Pickers and dealers aggressively ferreted out French bronzes by Lorenzl or silver tea sets by Puiforcat from amidst the clutter. Dusting and polishing these "found" objet d'art prizes, the new Deco middlemen upscaled the prices to meet the new demand on Madison Avenue.

Fine Deco artifacts such as glasswork by Lalique, metal-craft objects, screens, and console tables by Edgar Brandt, exquisite Chiparus and Preiss bronze-and-ivory Chryselephantine statuary, Dunand vases, or Ruhlmann furniture, which always were seen as highly crafted quality pieces, sold for top prices; but by today's standards they would seem to have gone for very little indeed. At the same time, American machine-produced tubular chrome furniture, Catalin jewelry, streamlined radio hardware, or blue- and peach-tinted designer wall mirrors and clocks were very inexpensive, and the early collector of this type of American Deco had a field day. For example, a carved Catalin horsehead brooch, which might today sell for $50 to $75 at a specialty dealer, could easily then be found for 25¢. Catalin and other plastic streamlined radios that could be bought for $25 now sell in the price range of $500 to $700 and up for the better examples. Frankart statuary, considered an oddity or pot-metal kitschy junk then, could be had for $5 and $10; the same pieces today sell for anywhere between $300 and $1,800. The dictum "today's junque may be tomorrow's treasure" was certainly the case for Deco in

Art Deco glazed-ceramic flower vase licensed by Walt Disney Productions in 1940 to commemorate Fantasia. The design features the goddess Artemis from the film's "Pastoral Symphony" segment. Manufactured by Vernon Kiln, California.

Roy Lichtenstein's Modern Painting Triptych II, 1967, oil and magna on canvas, collection of the artist. Photograph by Eric Pollitzer. (Courtesy of Leo Castelli Galleries, New York)

the late 1960s and the early 1970s. Those with a vision for this future-past style went to market with the fervor of archaeologists in search of treasures from a lost civilization. In this instance it was a search for pieces of a bygone age that appeared to be innocent compared to the chaos and upheaval inherent in the sixties. There was an awareness then that a cheap, disposable ethic was immanent, and many collectors sought to preserve relics from previous generations lest they disappear altogether in the trash pile. Many were looking for what they perceived to be a Lost America.

The style of the 1970s seemed primarily to reflect a wistful nostalgia for the period of early modernity. The revival of the 1925 musical *No, No Nanette* starring Ruby Keeler (of the Busby Berkeley–Warner Brothers musicals of the early 1930s) and with Berkeley directing opened as a big smash again on Broadway on January 19, 1970. Tap dancing, previously considered outmoded on the Great White Way, once again became the rage. Much of this was due to interest in the machine precision production numbers from the Berkeley films *42nd Street*, *Footlight Parade*, *Dames*, and the *Gold Digger* series of 1933, 1935, and 1937. Ginger Rogers and Fred Astaire pictures were also in vogue in the late sixties and the seventies; many were reprocessed by the studio and rereleased in bright new prints. Deco-cult movie audiences at first-run theaters and at revival houses applauded wildly after Fred and Ginger finished a jubilant or exotic dance routine in *Shall We Dance*, *The Gay Divorcee*, or *Top Hat*. An avid interest in the look of Deco-vamps like Garbo, Dietrich, or Harlow with their pencil-thin brows, false eyelashes, ruby-red lips, and pale white skin was also in fashion during this early Deco-revival period.

Harold Prince's *Follies*, another highly stylized

Statuette with Moderne features, bronze on onyx base, by French sculptor Lorenzl, ca. 1931.

Broadway musical in the nostalgic mood, starring Alexis Smith and Yvonne deCarlo, opened on Broadway in April of 1970. *Newsweek* of December 28, 1970, produced a cover issue for Christmas on "Nostalgia—The Vogue for the Old," which included stories on the big bands, old radio shows, vintage movies, the revival of Busby Berkeley films, and Berkeley's heralded direction of *No, No Nanette* on Broadway. In 1971 *Life* did a Valentine cover issue (February 19) featuring those old-time movie sweethearts on the cover, Rita Hayworth, Myrna Loy, Paulette Goddard, Betty Hutton, Joan Blondell, and—in the center of a big Deco heart—Ruby Keeler. The cover stated, "Everybody's talking about nostalgia." This *Life* special on the nostalgia wave featured articles with full-color spreads on *No, No Nanette*, Busby and his girls, gilded movie palaces, a fashion report called "Bright Lips of Yesterday," a story on the 1938 Orson Welles Martian invasion radio broadcast, a cover story on the old-time movie queens, and a personal view of "Nostalgia" penned by Loudon Wainwright. A highlight article on the Art Deco rage featured stunning full-size pictures of artifacts from the period, including a pair of 1920s pointed men's shoes with a sunburst design; a jazzy Deco enamel notepad cover; the Chrysler Building; an Art Deco porcelain coffee cup and saucer in gold, black, and green triangles with "Tango" orange flowers from Barbra Streisand's collection; a Jean Dunand crushed eggshell–lacquer vase; and a flamboyant 1930s statuette in carved ivory and silver of a snow queen with two polar bears standing on a white marble "ice" base from the collection of Ron Link.

One of the earliest important exhibitions of revival Art Deco was held at the Finch College Museum of Art on East 78th Street in New York City. The show ran from October 14 through November 30, 1970, and offered examples from many categories, including

Art Deco catalog from Finch College Museum of Art show, New York, 1970.

painting, sculpture, drawing, illustration, posters, bookbinding, books, jewelry, furniture, lamps, ceramics, glass, enamelware, silverware, and textiles. This show focused on many fine French Art Deco artifacts. Judith Applegate described Art Deco in the Finch catalog: "In its restless search for a direction and identity, Art Deco is a graphic manifestation of society's realization of the overwhelming changes that, with ever increasing acceleration, typify the twentieth century."

This show, arranged by Elayne H. Varian, traveled to the Cranbrook Academy of Art in Bloomfield Hills, Michigan, where it remained on view from January 19 through February 29, 1971.

There was also in 1971 a large Art Deco exhibition at the Minneapolis Institute of Art from July 8 through September 5. Guest-curated by Deco historian Bevis Hillier and coordinated by David Ryan, this exhibition contained 1,500 "authentic" objects, making it, according to the catalog, "the largest collection ever assembled." Art Deco pieces loaned by private dealers, institutions like Radio City Music Hall, and collectors like Barbra Streisand and Andy Warhol included furniture; ceramics; wood, metal, and enamel objects; textiles; jewelry; costumes; bookbindings; paintings; household accessories; and examples of Art Deco revival.

An exhibition, again entitled "Art Deco," opened in 1973 at the Museum of the State Historical Society of Wisconsin in Madison. This exhibition focused on a somewhat broader American interpretation of Deco. Joan Severa, the curator of this show, wrote in its brochure that Hollywood became a dominant cultural force in the 1930s since few could afford any other form of entertainment. Escapism to the movies offered millions living through a depression the opportunity to vicariously experience ultramodernity, glitter, glamour, haute couture, "Style Moderne" furniture, sleek bobs, and glistening makeup.

"When manufacturers developed the means to supply these items cheaply," Ms. Severa wrote, "American culture moved toward a futuristic, stylized, metallic, shining, colorful, fantastic environmental style that we now call Art Deco." The Wisconsin exhibition featured motion picture stills to back up its theme and also introduced cheaper American mass-production objects such as white-metal and plastic imitation Deco statuary, Lucite cigarette containers, spray-painted metal cigarette cases, torchère lamps, perfume bottles, and ready-made Sears-Roebuck-type moderne chrome and Naugahyde furniture. Even a Czechoslovakian import item made specifically for the American market, a 1930s ceramic wall plaque of a glamorous woman's head, and a German dress pin depicting a flapper walking her borzoi were included in the exhi-

Art Deco catalog from an exhibition at the Museum of the State Historical Society of Wisconsin, Madison, 1973.

bition to demonstrate the worldwide impact of Deco design. Many American-designed products were actually manufactured in foreign countries that offered the advantage of cheaper material and labor costs.

Other objects exhibited at the Wisconsin show included plaster incense burners with Egyptian motifs, a beaded woman's handbag selected to show American Indian influences on the mass market, Deco penny arcade slot machines, and examples of women's evening attire, daywear, and accessories from American fashion designers. Kitchenware was also included, e.g., aluminum kettles, sugar bowls and creamers, mixing bowls, tablecloths, and tea towels, all made in the U.S.A. Oddly enough, a category called "Men's Accessories" included among the Deco humidors, silk dressing gowns, and smoking jackets, this object description: "Radio. Mirror construction, blue with ebonized wood trim. Sparton, made by the

Sparks-Withington Company, Jackson, Michigan, ca. 1935."

Another movie came along in 1973 to add to the growing interest in things Deco. It was *Paper Moon*, filmed in black and white (just like a thirties movie) by Peter Bogdanovich and starring Ryan O'Neal, Madeline Kahn, and Tatum O'Neal. A slick con artist (Ryan) and a tough kid sidekick (Tatum) patterned after Little Orphan Annie and Jackie Coogan set up a number of bogus schemes in order to make it through the Depression. Bogdanovich used authentic 78 rpm records as background for his Deco-style movie. Audiences delighted in the sound of Jimmie Grier and his orchestra, Leo Reisman, Ozzie Nelson, Dick Powell, Paul Whiteman, the Boswell Sisters, and Enric Madriguera and his Hotel Biltmore Orchestra singing "Let's Have Another Cup of Coffee, Let's Have Another Piece of Pie." The 33⅓ rpm record from this picture created a

new interest in "nostalgia" or "Deco" music, and today record stores have entire sections devoted to the original classics from the golden era of radio and big bands and great performers. Though Billie Holiday, Mildred Bailey, and early Ella Fitzgerald have always been considered classics, now it is also Whispering Jack Smith, Ukelele Ike (Cliff Edwards), Dolly Dawn and her Dawn patrol, Ruth Etting, and Jack Hylton and his orchestra.

Another blockbuster Oscar-winning, Deco-period picture opened in 1973, *The Sting*, with Paul Newman and Robert Redford playing two sharp con artists involved in a Chicago confidence-game operation. Set in the 1930s, the movie was further evidence of the ongoing rage for nostalgia. Following this, in 1974, *The Great Gatsby*, based on the F. Scott Fitzgerald novel, starred Redford as Gatsby and Mia Farrow as Daisy. This picture, though not as financially successful as *The Sting*, caused a stir in the fashion world, particularly emphasizing 1920s styles for men and again feeding into the world of Art Deco, which by this time certainly could be regarded as one of the major style and decorative influences of this century. In a continuation of 1970s movies set in the Deco-period, the incorporation and enjoyment of things past helped to nurture, soothe, and balance the present, which seemed beset with more and more economic and social problems. Looking to the past seemed to provide a happier view toward the future.

In 1974–75 (from November 6 through January 5) Elayne H. Varian again mounted an exhibition, entitled "American Art Deco Architecture," at the Finch College Museum of Art. Covering everything from New York skyscrapers, terra-cotta ornamentation, metal grillwork, interiors and exteriors of movie theaters and restaurants, building lobbies and ornate bronze mailboxes, elevator doors and terrazzo floors, this

Cobalt blue glazed-ceramic refrigerator jug by Hall China for Westinghouse.

photographic show, with some illustrations and drawings, helped to open up the awareness of Art Deco landmarks from one end of the country to the other.

In the November 11, 1974, issue of trendsetting *New York* magazine, the style-conscious weekly periodical featured a cover story called "Art Deco's Back and New York's Got It," with a subtitle "The Latest Word about the Latest Look." A model sporting a sculptured hairdo, smoking a cigarette in a long cigarette holder, and posing against a chrome Deco wall sculpture is on the cover. This issue was filled to the brim with enthusiasm for Deco; the lead article by Anne Hollander had a subheading that declared, "Whether or not you can remember its original impact, the style strikes the authentic note of chic in today's marketplace. . . ." An article by Dorothy Seiberling was entitled "New York Is a Deco Spectacle," with the subheading, "Thanks to a construction boom that began around 1925, hundreds of Deco-style buildings went up all over the city. . . ." This article praised the Chrysler Building at length and had splendid color photographs by Stan Shaffer of the steamship-modern interior of the side-entrance hallway of the Hotel Edison, built in 1931; the Chanin Building on 42nd Street; Bloomingdale's department store; the Western Union building; and several 1930s apartment buildings in the Bronx. In the same issue an amusing article by art critic David Bourdon was entitled, "Stacking the Deco," with the subheading, "For the past ten years Andy Warhol has been buying up Deco objects, from unabashed kitsch to the rare and exquisite. . . ."

Apparently Warhol might spend anywhere from $5 for a trinket to $1,500 for an object/treasure without the blink of a silver eyelash. A photo displayed more than forty ceramic streamlined icebox pitchers and butter dishes. Another photo showed a "Deco-bedecked" Andy sporting his "early plastic" jewelry.

Bourdon noted that Warhol would haunt certain shops until he depleted their stock, storing his Deco finds in warehouses. When Warhol was asked to estimate how many tens of thousands of dollars he had spent on Deco, his feigned reply was, "I can't put it in terms of money. It's my *life*."

Subsequent issues of *New York* that highlighted the Deco revival with cover stories were September 15, 1975 ("*Gold Diggers of 1975*—A Nostalgic Look for Fall"), December 29, 1975 ("You Oughta Be in Pictures," an account of New York City in black-and-white Deco musicals, in disaster movies, and crime movies), and December 20, 1976 ("Art Deco Empire Diner").

In addition to the release of *Chinatown*, which was set in 1937 in Los Angeles and featured Faye Dunaway and Jack Nicholson, 1974 was also the year of the first Art Deco "show" at the greatest Art Deco palace of them all, Radio City Music Hall. From January 30 through February 3, 1974, Radio City was host to the New York Art Deco Exposition, featuring Deco wares from all over the country exhibited by forty-two dealers spread out over the grand foyer and downstairs lounge of the venerable picture palace. On display outside the theater was a 1936 Hudson Hornet used in *The Godfather* and a 1937 Dodge cab. Thirty-five thousand people paid $3.50 each to shop for Deco teapots, wallpaper, bronze statuary, Chase chrome, or fine French Deco jewelry. The admission price also included the viewing of such pictures as *Top Hat* (1935) and *Swing Time* (1936) with Fred Astaire and Ginger Rogers, the original uncut version of *King Kong* (1933), and *She* (1935) with Helen Gahagan and Randolph Scott. Aside from these four, most of the other pictures shown during the exposition were not "Deco," though a *March of Time* newsreel included with each screening provided authentic period detail.

An excellent film program was featured in July, 1974, at San Francisco's International Art Deco Exhibition. Chosen by filmmaker Kenneth Anger, with the assistance of Tom Luddy of the Pacific Film Archives, the films included such rarely seen treasures as *Our Modern Maidens* (1929), Joan Crawford's last silent, with sets by Cedric Gibbons; *Madame Satan* (1929, Cecil B. DeMille), featuring a ballet in a dirigible struck by lightning; Ziegfeld's *Glorifying the American Girl* and *Reaching for the Moon* (1931) with Douglas Fairbanks and Bebe Daniels, with sets of the "Ritzbilt Hotel" and a luxury ocean liner by William Cameron Menzies. Other special movie treats at this West Coast exhibition included *Paramount on Parade*; Garbo's last silent, *The Kiss*; Mitchell Leisen's *Murder at the Vanities* (1934), which includes the musical numbers "The Rape of the Rhapsody" and "Sweet Marijuana"; chapters of *Flash Gordon* with Buster Crabbe; and compilations of Busby Berkeley musical numbers.

The 1975 New York Art Deco Exposition at Radio City Music Hall ran from January 28 through February 2. Many dealers in fine Art Deco participated in this second show at Radio City, which went a long way in educating the public as to exactly what Art Deco was. A special exhibit on the mezzanine level of the Music Hall featured World's Fair memorabilia from the collection of Larry Zim. Another exhibit featured Art Deco room settings with a "Hollywood Moderne" wood-and-mohair armchair, a chrome-and-ebony RCA Victor console radio John Vassos designed, and a porcelain enamel kitchen table from the executive's commissary of the New York World's Fair of 1939, with four wooden chairs all featuring the Fair's symbol, the Trylon and Perisphere. A tubular neon orange-and-blue Trylon and Perisphere topped this exhibition, glowing out over the grand foyer of the Hall.

Deco featured at this significant show included

New York Art Deco Exposition at Radio City Music Hall, catalog published by Big Apple Events, Inc., 1975.

bronze medallions, Lucite table lamps, Frankart mood lamps, rare handmade ceramics, a Clarice Cliff tea set, silver tea sets, Lalique glass, smoking accessories, Catalin jewelry, collector books, paintings, lithographs by Louis Icart (exhibited by a specialist with the amusing pseudonym Arthur Deco, whose studio on East 13th Street in New York was called The Art Deco Center of America), textiles, radios, and hundreds of other examples of good Deco design. Signs of Deco items' being reproduced for a new market in the seventies were apparent at this last Deco exhibition at Radio City Music Hall, including vases from the Contemporary Arts Glass Group and decorative sand-etched mirrors from the Narcissus Mirror Company. A dealer from Philadelphia called "Rosebud" produced replicas of Deco-style painted-on-reverse glass stand-up picture frames for the table or vanity.

The film program at this second exhibition was a great improvement over the first. It included *Metropolis* (1926) accompanied by Lee Erwin on the Radio City organ; *Blonde Venus* (1932) directed by Josef von Sternberg with Marlene Dietrich and Cary Grant; *Platinum Blonde* (1931) with Jean Harlow; *Trouble in Paradise* (1932) with Miriam Hopkins; *Midnight* (1939) with Claudette Colbert; *Shall We Dance* (1937); *Poor Little Rich Girl* (1936) with Shirley Temple and Alice Faye; *Wake Up and Live* (1937) with Alice Faye, Ben Bernie, and Walter Winchell; *Twentieth Century* (1934) with Carole Lombard and John Barrymore; and *His Girl Friday* (1939) with Rosalind Russell and Cary Grant. Each film showing was accompanied by a Fox Movietone newsreel from the 1930s. Audiences thrilled to see these movies on the big screen at Radio City; it is unfortunate that more revival films cannot be shown in this splendid Art Deco environment. Thanks to the attention drawn to the Music Hall by these two exhibitions and other special programs, the venerable

Deco palace was saved from destruction in 1982.

By the 1980s the awareness of Art Deco as a unique and important modernistic style had spread across the country. Many major cities formed Art Deco societies with active and prominent leaders and charter members determined to identify and protect buildings and (sometimes) their interiors, demanding recognition for them as valuable architectural treasures of the twentieth century. Art Deco societies conduct lecture series, document historical information (often from persons involved in the original movement who are still living), arrange exhibitions, sponsor city walking tours, and create annual events like the Art Deco shows and festivals where restricted merchandise is sold by important dealers and collectors.

Early 1970s business cards. Deco was a smart shop at 19 Christopher Street in Greenwich Village, and Arthur Deco was the name taken by the proprietor for the Art Deco Center of America, which was located at 17 East 13th Street, New York. Robert Flinn designed the card for Deco on Christopher Street.

Original poster design by Dennis Abbe for the Art Deco Society of New York, mixed media on paper, ca. 1983.

Silk-screened party-invitation card printed in France, late 1920s.

On the fun-life-style side of it there are the Deco balls and parties held in Art Deco hotels like the Waldorf-Astoria on Park Avenue, aboard luxury liners, or in fashionable nightclubs like the Rainbow Room atop Rockefeller Center. Often vintage cars deliver gentlemen in tuxedoes and high hats and ladies in streamlined thirties gowns and white fox furs. A small dance orchestra playing the old tunes, Deco decorations, and bubbly champagne help to recapture the spirit of a bygone time when a night on the town was just the thing to chase away Depression blues. The musical *42nd Street*, based on the Busby Berkeley film and with splendid Art Deco sets and costumes, has tap-tap-tapped its way through to the nineties, in New York, London, and elsewhere, contributing to the idea that Deco is here to stay. Following that musical, David Merrick revived Gershwin's *Oh, Kay* for a new audience.

Furthering the interest in things Deco, the 1980s started out with a bang with the founding of the Art Deco Society of New York and a rash of large and small exhibitions and shows. Although not every show connected to Art Deco can be mentioned here, we have tried to concentrate on the most exemplary or important ones.

In 1981 the Delaware Art Museum in Wilmington mounted a show called "Consumer's Choice: The American Home 1890–1940," from February 8 through April 19. Curator Elizabeth Hawkes showed a sampling of the mass-produced objects that people bought for their homes—specifically those things widely affordable or that could be purchased on the installment plan. The highlight of the show was four room settings: a kitchen and parlor from 1915 and a kitchen and living room from 1935 furnished with authentic and exemplary household objects in the context of the home.

New York's first Art Deco Weekend, in June 1983, sponsored by the Art Deco Society of New York, drew 2,000 people to a show and sale at the original McGraw-Hill Building on West 42nd Street. A sale of Art Deco objects by prominent dealers was a feature as well as lectures on diverse Deco topics by leading authorities.

The 1984 Art Deco Week, also sponsored by the New York society, was an even greater success than the previous year. The show and sale were held in Walter Chrysler's private (men only) Cloud Club in the spire of the Chrysler Building on the sixty-sixth and sixty-seventh floors. There were other events, including lectures and walking tours followed by a gala dance in the lobby of the Chrysler Building.

The 1985 event was also held in the Cloud Club and drew thousands of Art Deco enthusiasts who lined up around the block to get a glimpse of the legendary Cloud Club rooms, which had been closed for over a decade. The 1985 festivities, which included lectures,

Promotion booklet, Miami Beach, 1982. Published by Community Action and Research, project director Paul Rothman, graphics Woody Vondracek.

walking tours, fashion shows, and a Deco ball, celebrated the sixtieth anniversary of the 1925 Paris Exposition of Modern Decorative and Industrial Arts. At the gala opening festivities, Michael Love, then president of the society, said, "It's really the last of the true styles—it touches every element of life. . . ." William Weber, the society's president emeritus, said, in referring to Art Deco's enduring appeal, "It's elegant and it's kitsch . . . it's appealing to the young and the old alike. It's exuberant, but also refined."

In September 1985, the Whitney Museum's show "High Style: 20th Century American Design," opened in New York. Filled with utilitarian Deco objects rather than high art, the exhibition prompted *New York* magazine art critic Kay Larson to make the following comments: "In an industrial society, design is the means by which art enters ordinary lives—a transaction as complicated and value-laden as the capitalism that spawned it. . . . The problem . . . is not with the design itself, but with the museum's role in certifying commodity culture—reinforcing the recent urge to award a high value to 'the most important, the ultra-fashionable, the unusually dramatic'—and the extraordinarily well-off." She also said, in complimenting the curators at the Whitney, that "the usual decorative arts department of a museum is filled with relics of earlier centuries; archaeological as well as aesthetic objects distant enough in time and space to be immune to salesmanship. . . ."

Fifty-two years after the Museum of Modern Art presented an exhibition called "Machine Art," the Brooklyn Museum in 1986 mounted a show curated by Dianne Pilgrim and Richard Guy Wilson called "The Machine Age in America, 1918–1941." As noted in our preface, this show was designed to travel to different locations around the country and undoubtedly contributed a great deal to an understanding of

Altman magazine for fall and winter of 1931 catalogued "the correct style" in fashion for madame, misses, gentlemen, young girls and boys, and "wee tots," plus outfits for maids and home nurses. Deco gift items, novelties, and jewelry were also offered by one of the greatest of New York department stores.

Main lounge, San Francisco Stock Exchange, 1930, architects Timothy L. Pflueger and James R. Miller.

the impact that industry (and industrial designers) had on the American consciousness in the 1920s and 1930s. The exhibition contained examples of architectural renderings, photographs, prints and original art, clothing, textiles, furniture, lighting fixtures, glass, and ceramics. The crowd-pleasing showstoppers, however, were typical American household objects, many designed by leading designers, including a Sears-Roebuck Silvertone radio, a Waring Blendor, a Raymond Loewy pencil sharpener, a Donald Deskey table-top lamp, a Henry Dreyfuss refrigerator, a dozen Gilbert Rohde table clocks, a Walter Dorwin Teague camera, Russel Wright bookends, an Electrolux vacuum cleaner, coffee urns and tea sets by Manning Bowman and Chase Brass and Copper Company, cigarette cases and lighters, and Catalin, Bakelite, and Marblette jewelry.

In 1986, at the Park Avenue Armory (November 20–23), antiques impresario Sanford Smith mounted the first annual Modernism show, an exhilarating display of American and European furnishings exhibited by some of the world's leading dealers. Included in this first show were objects covering a century of design from the Aesthetic Movement and the Bauhaus to Art Nouveau and Art Deco. Of special interest was a handmade Paul Frankl Skyscraper bookcase in redwood selling for $90,000, suites of Frank Lloyd Wright furniture, lamps, and leaded glass, a 9-by-12-foot wool rug from the Grand Foyer of Radio City Music Hall, a Mies van der Rohe 1929 Barcelona chair, and a wide variety of unique, one-of-a-kind jukeboxes and console radios.

The Smithsonian Institution's National Museum of American Art opened its exhibition called "American Art Deco" at the newly restored Renwick Gallery on April 17, 1987, where it remained on view through July 17, 1987, before traveling to the Center for Fine Arts in Miami, the Joslyn Art Museum in Omaha, Nebraska, the Philbrook Museum of Art in Tulsa, Oklahoma, and the Minnesota Museum of Art in St. Paul. This show, curated by Alastair Duncan, featured 180 of the finest examples of good Art Deco design in furniture, ceramics, glass, sculpture, textiles, silver, and small decorative objects, all chosen to illustrate the considerable transformation that resulted from the style's transatlantic journey.

Dungeon Deco: bronze "Administration" sign from the reception rotunda of the demolished House of Detention for Women, Greenwich Village, New York City, Sloan and Robertson, architects, 1931. This bronze sign, along with two others from the House of Detention, was exhibited at the American Art Deco Show at the Smithsonian Institution's National Gallery of Art, Renwick Gallery, Washington, D.C., and traveled with the show to various American cities.

Deco Life-styles

The times we live in today allow many people to choose whatever life-style or decade suits their fantasy. In fact, it is easier to lead a Deco life-style now than it would have been in the late 1920s or in the long ten years of the Great Depression. Many young people are doing just that, but not in nostalgic reverie for the past, since most of them were not born until after World War II. Sometime in the 1970s, all the decades of the modern era—the 1920s, '30s, '40s, '50s, and '60s—seemed to coalesce, one on top of the other, like a Dagwood sandwich of nostalgia. The 1970s, more than any other earlier decade in this country, was a period in which we looked to what appeared to be, from a distance, safer and more secure times. In selecting from the brighter elements of the past, we could, it seems, see life in a rosier hue, as the lyric from the old song says, "I'm looking at the world through rose-colored glasses—and everything is rosy now!" The Ronald Reagan–dominated 1980s will also be remembered as a decade in which we looked with wistful longing to the past for familiar values that, once disengaged or lost, are not easily reasserted. The 1990s seem to be according twentieth-century movements such as Art Deco classic status.

The *San Francisco Focus* magazine of February 1985, in a cover article by Leslie Harlib called "Past Perfect," reported that the Bay Area was then in the

Jell-o desserts in the 1930s were often turned out of elaborate Art Deco molds in stainless steel or aluminum and presented with fanfare at the

Depression-era kitchen table. This 1937 radio send-away Jell-o Recipe booklet from General Foods Corp., featuring Jack Benny and Mary

Livingston, is filled with fanciful, colorful Jell-o Deco desserts.

midst of an all-out Art Deco revival. In laid-back California style, it seems that many San Franciscans were creating for themselves an all-encompassing environment filled with the romance and gracious living of a lost era.

One of those involved in this magnificent obsession is Laurie Gordon, who appears to have stepped right out of a Varga calendar. In a talk with Ms. Gordon, who has served as president of the San Francisco Art Deco Society, we learned that her coterie of Deco devotees not only decorate their apartments in thirties style but neither own television sets or listen to rock music. Instead, they play only old 78 rpm records on Deco Victrolas. Living rooms are often painted a soft peach accented with blue mirror and glass brick, while lighting is always indirect Lumalite, unless one is able to find original Mazda-lite bulbs from the thirties.

Kitchens are often painted a Depression green (a sort of grayish Nile green) or deep cream. Dishware is either Fiesta or translucent green, pink, yellow, red, or blue Depression glass, which originally was sold at the dime store. In the 1930s many fine Deco items were found for a nickel or a dime at Woolworth's or McCrory's, particularly for the kitchen. Preferred toasters brown only one side at a time, and San Franciscans known to carry things to the extreme transfer their mayonnaise into old Hellman's jars and put their ground coffee into 1930s Bokar tins.

"We are very into Deco foods such as Jell-o molded into the shape of Aztec temples," Laurie informed us, "and Spam is definitely on our list. We drink only electro-perked coffee—from an Art Deco coffee urn, of course. We also like to use vintage waffle irons, and we decant our syrup into Log Cabin Syrup tins in the log cabin shape—or if that seems too impractical, into a Fiesta-ware syrup dispenser."

San Francisco Art Deco Weekend by the Bay program, 1986.

Picking up a 1930s *Good Housekeeping* magazine from Laurie Gordon's blue-mirrored coffee table, we noticed that in the food advertisements a great deal of concern was paid to home economics and a housewife's budget, probably because so many people were on the dole. It was suggested to mothers that they serve, for instance, meatloaf with Del Monte canned peas on Thursdays and Heinz baked beans with grilled frankfurters on Saturdays. On Friday night American mothers could whip up a batch of Depression doughnuts (made from scratch and deep-fried in Spry) to keep the family satisfied while they tuned into their favorite radio program on the big Deco console in the living room. Ovaltine served in a Little Orphan Annie Beetleware shake-up mug sufficed for the children while mom and dad drank A & P percolator coffee.

"The sixties flower kids told us, 'Do your own thing,' and that's exactly what we're doing. For me, it's not the 'Lifestyles of the Rich and Famous,'" says Laurie Gordon, "it's just Deco, Deco, and more Deco." Her favorite Deco dish? An ice-cream sundae made with black raspberry and pistachio ice cream, covered with chocolate and marshmallow toppings, a mound of whipped cream, a splash of chopped nuts, topped by a maraschino cherry, and served in a high-standing vessel. "Just the taste will remind you of the Deco era," Ms. Gordon assured us as we sat and watched her daintily spoon this concoction into her mouth in an old-fashioned soda fountain–candy shop in the Haight-Ashbury district of San Francisco, a city that seriously treasures its past.

Designs for Living, *1930s booklet from the Studio of Creative Design, Pittsburgh Plate Glass Company.*

THE MODERN HOME

In 1926 a traveling exhibition of selected Deco items from the Paris exposition of 1925 toured eight American cities, including Boston, and it eventually arrived at the all-important Metropolitan Museum of Art in New York. Entitled "The International Exposition of Modern Decorative and Industrial Art," it gave the American public a chance to view modernistic French-manner *décoratifs* that included designs by Edgar Brandt and Jean Dunand. Initially the American press had been contemptuous of this display of modernism, which they considered vulgar, but department stores competed eagerly to capitalize on what was believed to be an exciting new trend in furnishings and objects. Though bored with the stilted, traditionalist look of the rooms they had lived in for too many years, many chagrined customers were either bewildered or awe-struck as they examined, for the first time out of the movies, a modern decorative arrangement stated in twentieth-century terminology.

By 1928 there had been as many as fifty different exhibitions of modern rooms in museums or in department stores across the country. Stores like L. Bamberger's and Hahnes in Newark, Marshall Field in Chicago, Wanamakers in Philadelphia and New York, and the City of Paris in San Francisco all showed modern interiors in their furniture departments. Clearly a new trend in buying and selling was at hand for what was then usually referred to by sales personnel as "Art Moderne." In February of 1928 Lord & Taylor on Fifth Avenue presented an "exposition of Modern French Decorative Art," showing the store's own designs of several innovative model rooms right alongside styles dictated by the French-manner school of Art Deco. In May 1928, R. H. Macy & Co. in New York followed with their "Art in Trade Exposition," featuring fifteen model rooms decorated by European and American designers like Bruno Paul, Kem Weber, and Gio Ponti.

White painted brick with black streamlined trim, glass brick, and polished-aluminum details combined in a fine example of the Depression-modern architectural style espoused at the Century of Progress Exposition in 1933. Private home, Chicago suburbs, ca. mid-1930s.

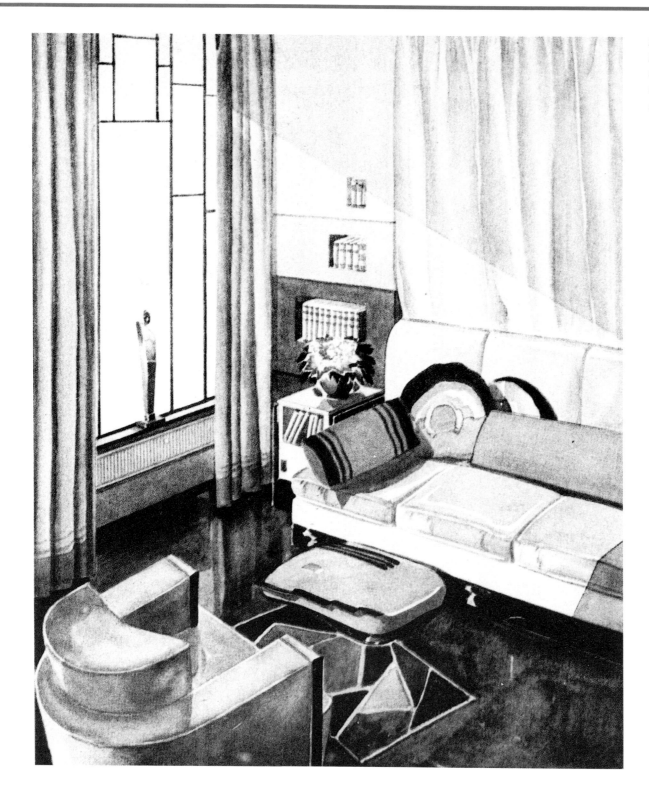

Deco-interior illustration for
Herman Nelson Invisible Radiators: ''See if you can locate the heating unit.''
Architecture, *July 1929.*

Armstrong Linoleum floor advertisement showing geometric-patterned linoleum with Deco-style rattan furnishings for the sun room. Home Furnishing Arts, *spring 1933.*

Room for progressive moderns featuring chrome furniture, from Home Furnishing Arts, *fall and winter, 1934.*

held in the Chase Bank Building on 57th Street in Manhattan, that a second was presented by the same group in 1929 with notable examples of lamps, vases, and wall sconces exhibited. At this show the entire decorative scheme of the room and its contents were available for sale to the public.

An exhibition called "The Architect and the Industrial Arts" was held at the Metropolitan Museum of Art in 1929. Major American designers like Ely-Jacque Kahn, Raymond Hood, Eliel Saarinen, and Joseph Urban here focused on materials new to the decorative arts, such as aluminum, Vitrolite glass, reinforced rubber, rayon textiles, and other synthetics. Over 140 industrial-mode designers and craftsmen and nine participating architects led to the success of this modernistic show, which was viewed with a new objectivity when the public saw it within the context of a major museum.

By autumn of that year, the American Designers Gallery, a group of men that included Donald Deskey, Joseph Urban, Wolfgang Hoffman, Raymond Hood, and over two dozen other noted designers and architects, arranged a display of ten decorated rooms and a number of side attractions devoted simply to new Deco object forms. So successful was this display,

Kresge "Home in the Sky" souvenir matchbook. Message inside reads: "A pre-fabricated modern home, à poem in streamline steel, beautifully landscaped and erected on the roof of the Kresge Department Store, designed for the family of moderate income and completely furnished in the modern manner by Kresge interior decorators." Kresge Department Store, Newark, New Jersey, 1934.

Art Deco floral-patterned rug runner. (Cadillac Jack, Hollywood, California)

Deco theater carpeting by Wilton Company manufactured in 27 in. widths and laid wall to wall in movie theaters during the 1930s. (First ½, Soho, New York City)

Bright and colorful vat-dyed floral upholstery, drapery, pillow, and slipcover fabrics extremely popular and practical in home decor during the 1930s, '40s, and '50s. Illustrated booklet from Waverly Bonded Fabric Company of New York, late 1930s.

Depression room installation with overstuffed maroon velour chair, floor lamp with fringed shade, wallpaper, ashtray, blue-mirrored coffee table, telephone, console radio, circular peach-colored wall mirror, and boy's pedal car, from "Consumers Choice: The American Home, 1890–1940," Delaware Art Museum, 1981.

3-Pcs. STREAMLINED MODERN SUITE

In a word . . . exquisite! The striped mohair covering is soft and silky. Well proportioned pieces that form the basis for a model room. Note the curved back Master Club Chair. Super Sagless. $149

★ ★ ★

3-Pcs. GENUINE MOHAIR FRIEZE

For those who prefer the conventional period style, this handsome carved frame suite covered in genuine Mohair Frieze is an outstanding value, Super-Sagless. All three pieces. 5 year moth guarantee. $98

ern Art, under the aegis of Philip Johnson, held an exhibition that oddly set Art Nouveau and Art Deco in direct relationship, as if one were meant to complement the other. This idea of interrelating these two forms confused the public, who did not take well to this particular exhibition.

By 1934 the ground was broken with a highly regarded and successful show at the Museum of Modern Art entitled "Machine Art" (also curated by twenty-eight-year-old Philip Johnson), which presented everything from home furnishings, including modern accessories for the living room, bedroom, and kitchen, to units for a more modern and efficient office. The

Summer rug of Kraft fiber with a circular and geometric design, Waite Carpet Company, 12 x 6 ft., ca. 1930.

Metropolitan Museum of Art booklet from "The Architect and the Industrial Arts" exhibition of contemporary American design, 1929.

With the onslaught of the market crash in October 1929 and the bleak, early years of the Depression that followed, the modern movement became firmly entrenched as the style that brought with it a forward-looking trend and a sense of hope for the future in the midst of black despair. In 1933, which many historians now refer to as the worst year of the Great Depression—a year that also found Franklin Delano Roosevelt taking office, Hitler becoming chancellor of the Third Reich, Prohibition ending, and the National Recovery Act going into effect—the Museum of Mod-

clean line and functionalism of design at this influential exhibition helped open the public's eyes to the aesthetics of the new modern age that was clearly heading their way.

Also in 1934 the Metropolitan Museum of Art held an all-important exhibition of contemporary American industrial art with more than 230 entries. The museum required all artifacts and furnishings contributed to the show to be original and created with the idea in mind of mass-production manufacturing.

This industrial art show, perhaps more than any other, led to the opening of many small retail shops, such as Modernage at 162 East 33rd Street, Doehler Metal Furniture Company on Lexington Avenue at 32nd Street, New Mode Furniture at 342 East 38th Street, Joseph Aronson, Inc., at 215 East 58th Street, and others. These shops offered tubular-steel chromium furniture of sturdy construction and high-quality modern design, custom upholstered furniture, tables, mirrors, lamps, rugs, and accessories as well as personal decorating services to customers who wanted to "go Moderne" in the 1930s.

Many household and home-decorating magazines of the period such as *Arts and Decoration*, *House Beautiful*, *House and Garden*, and *Home Furnishings* began to publish feature articles with photographic studies of fashionable, streamlined room settings that were easy to maintain, free of clutter, and stripped of excess ornamentation.

Modernism, as we think of it today when looking at the simplified high-tech interiors in the *New York Times* "Home" section, was originally very slow to enter into the American home, whose inhabitants still preferred a clumsy, overstuffed chair to its sleek chrome and leather counterpart. However, much of the modish 1930s chromium furniture did turn up in doctors' or dentists' waiting rooms, in beauty parlors,

This painted plaster "Dagwood Bumstead" Deco vase could be purchased at F. W. Woolworth's in the late 1920s.

Colorful Deco "Royal Art Pottery" vase made in England.

This skyscraper Deco "tango"-orange flower vase of thick-glazed ceramic came in three sizes. They can be found in a multicolor glaze as well as in solid colors, usually orange and green. Manufactured by the Pfaltzgraff Pottery Co. of York, Pennsylvania, 1930s.

The Red Room Grill, an Avondale Dairy store that was located in Allentown, Pennsylvania. C. T. Art Colortone postcard.

Installation of a complete ice-cream parlor luncheonette from the 1930s. Moderne-style Catalin, wood, and chrome jukebox, glass-brick wall panel, chrome and black Formica tables and leatherette chairs and counter stools complete this nostalgic setting. (Depression Modern, Soho, New York City)

Inside cover of a matchbook depicting the lunch counter of the Central YMCA in Philadelphia, Pennsylvania, ca. 1935.

bakeries, restaurants, nightclubs, or offices revamped by commercial construction companies.

Middle-class homes in the Depression that still featured "Humperdinck Gingerbread" ornamentation for dining room sets might well have had a porcelain-enamel table and chairs with bent tubular chrome legs in the kitchen. The new industrial household objects designed by Harold Van Doren, Loewy, Teague, Dreyfuss, Bel Geddes, and Rohde, including toasters, mixers, and other appliances, baby table-radios, and the cocktail shaker, usually joined an eclectic mix of various period styles in the American home, which always has leaned closer to comfort than to design concepts pleasing to the more sophisticated eye.

On the other hand, apartment dwellers were quick to utilize modern unit furniture in order to organize and simplify limited space. As early as 1927 Paul Frankl designed his skyscraper bookcases that, "moving upward" through stepped-up, setback progressions, were just like the towering structures of New York City. Many reinterpretations and home-craftsman versions of Frankl's bookcases were made in the 1930s for use in the modern den or living room.

The home bar, if not a separate room, was sometimes to be found in the cellar of a house or at one end, or "nook," of the parlor. The actual bar was often purchased at a specialty furniture or department store, or it was built at home from a shop-manual instruction booklet. In the Streamline Moderne curvilinear style, with glass bricks or tubular neon, recessed lighting, and chromium trim around a Formica countertop, these units were often a family's first piece of modernistic household furniture. After 1933 and the repeal of Prohibition, many gathered around their newly acquired status symbol—the portable bar—sitting on high, swivel, chrome-and-leatherette barstools, sipping fancy mixed drinks in small chro-

Modernage advertisement, 1935.

Dansley Modern Furniture ad from Arts and Decoration, March 1935.

Opposite: Doehler, and Home-craft Studios advertisements from Arts and Decoration magazine, February 1935; and Kochs Chrometal advertise-ment for beauty shops, ca. 1930s.

Arts and Decoration, Febru-ary 1935.

Popular Home Craft, September–October 1934, showing "build-it-yourself" skyscraper-style modernistic magazine case.

House Beautiful, City House and Apartment issue, Novem-ber 1931.

mium tumblers poured from a chromium and Catalin cocktail shaker. These elegant metal bar-sets were manufactured by Chase Brass and Copper Company, Revere Copper and Brass Company, West Bend Aluminum Company, or Manning Bowman and many other firms that hired industrial designers to lend a sense of "the modern" to post-Prohibition drinking. Also available for the bar were cocktail trays, peanut bowls, and hors d'oeuvre and snack trays, as well as other novelty bar knickknacks like the oddball toothpick olive/cheese retainers that were in the shapes of cranes or penguins.

The elegant cocktail party came to replace the need for wild all-night "bathtub gin" binges and Gatsby-style house parties so popular in the roaring twenties. Usually held from five to seven o'clock, to cater to working schedules, this prolonged "Happy

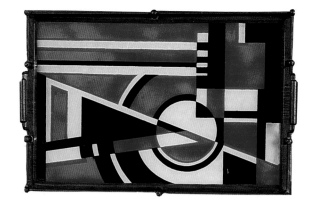

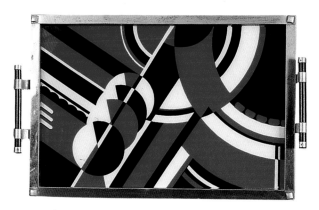

Cocktail serving trays in many striking design variations were a celebration of the end of Prohibition. Painted-on-reverse glass and chromium cocktail trays in distinctive Jazz-Deco patterns, ca. 1934.

Dime store Deco painted-on-reverse glass stand-up frame with tinted photo of movie star Marion Davies.

Town and Country, *May 15, 1934, ad for International Silver Company of Meriden, Connecticut. Post-Prohibition silver-plated cocktail shaker designed by Lurelle Guild.*

Bar countertop, wall paneling, and mural in Sealex Wall Linoleum for a modern-style family bar room, den, or cellar rumpus room in a small home. From Sealex Linoleum brochure, 1937. Chase Brass and Copper Company bar accessories complete the picture.

Hour'' pattern was also established at finer cocktail "lounges" (often just newly opened and decorated in the Depression-Moderne style of the 1930s), the corner tavern, or at the fancier hotel nightclubs.

Today the interest in 1930s mass-produced tubular chromium furniture is at an all-time high. Streamlined metal furnishings such as coffee, or cocktail, tables, with black glass or red, green, or black lacquered or Formica tops, torchère floor lamps, couches and chairs with leather or "leatherette" upholstery, cabinets, side tables, standing ashtrays, and other occasional furniture create a light airy feeling; they fit in easily alongside today's newer modern-design interpretations.

One major company that produced chromium furni-

Green glass-brick bar with chrome stools, in model modern room at Bloomingdale's department store featuring painting by Philip Nogga. Pictured in Arts and Decoration, March 1935.

Evercraft chromium cocktail shaker with chrome-metal cocktail glasses by Chase Brass and Copper Company, ca. 1934.

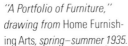

"A Portfolio of Furniture," drawing from Home Furnishing Arts, *spring–summer 1935.*

Bird's-eye view of fanciful "Repeal" cocktail room featuring painted mural decorations, electric refrigerator, sink, recessed glass shelves, and chromium bar stools, in Home Furnishing Arts, *spring 1933.*

Green lacquer and silver metal table, ca. 1930.

glass container were available in a variety of styles, as were kitchen and bridge table-and-chair sets, desks, vanities, and half-moon chrome-framed mirrors.

Royalchrome's cold-rolled tubular steel was first copper plated, then nickel plated, and then chromium plated and buffed. Leatherette used for covering chairs and couches was called Tuf-Tex and was available in Jasper green, beige, Florentine blue, Harlequin red, gloss black, rust, antique ivory, and a rust orange. Royaloid Formica tabletops came in verde antique, black and gold, Chinese red, and black. It should be noted that furniture of tubular chrome offered at department stores today often lacks the weight, sturdiness, or quality of a similar Deco-period original.

A modernist living room of the Depression era would also have geometric-patterned rugs, wallpaper, and draperies, which might feature Picasso-like de-

ture, the Royal Metal Manufacturing Company, had its main showroom in Chicago, with branches in New York, Pittsburgh, and Boston, and factories in Michigan City, Indiana, New York City, Los Angeles, and in Toronto, Canada. This company, which produced a distinctive furniture line called Royalchrome, sold two- and three-cushioned settees, a vast array of chairs, and endless assorted pedestal tables, cocktail and coffee tables with round, square, or oblong tops furnished with alcohol-resistant black-lacquered wood. They also were sold with Royaloid tops, a one-inch, nine-ply, built-up Formica product with polished aluminum edging. Smokers, smoking tables, and coffee tables equipped with chromium-topped ashtrays that had flippers that deposited ashes into a removable

Chrome and leather industrial-design chair made for beauty parlors, offices, restaurants, and for the modern home.

Lyn Colby

Sears Home Furnishing Adviser

Lyn Colby, an authority on Interior Decoration, has been retained by *Sears* to help you select furnishings for a more beautiful home.

Perhaps you have dreamed of having a real interior decorator give you suggestions on color harmony and balance of design, so that your home would be the pride of your family—and win the admiration of all who visit you. Lyn Colby will make that dream come true. The stunning effects she attains by combining pieces from *Sears* catalog has made her a popular friend of hundreds of our customers. She will advise you, too, if you wish.

Just fill out the coupon on opposite page!

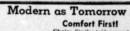

Modern chrome furnishings featured in Sears, Roebuck catalog, 1934.

Black lacquer and chrome end table. Chrometube by Paidar, ca. 1930s.

signs or floral patterns of tropical flowers, birds, or Chinese bridges and Japanese pagodas. A vase, clock, light fixture, or other decorative object had to be "moderne" or Deco, and such items were all mass produced for a burgeoning new modern marketplace.

Large, circular blue, peach-pink, yellow, or chartreuse mirrors were used for decorative accents. False-Moderne-style fireplaces meant to "center" a room were painted cream (sometimes blue mirror was glued to the surfaces), with streamlines of thin metal strips and glass brick lit from behind. These often had hidden compartments on the side or in the mantel tops that kept liquor bottles and cocktail glasses from view. This all-purpose mystery furniture was for those who did not care to sit around the home bar, who still wanted to distance themselves from alcohol. Many an occasional drinker had become used to hiding bottles under the kitchen sink during Prohibition. Novelty

Howell Chromsteel Furniture shown at the Chicago Century of Progress Exposition, 1933. Home Furnishing Arts, fall and winter, 1934.

Art Deco woven-cotton drapery fabric.

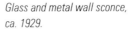

Glass and metal wall sconce, ca. 1929.

WPA-style lamps of gray-glazed ceramic-on-wood with fiberglass shades, ca. 1938. The pair are attributed to Russel Wright.

radios like the Pla-Pal, with concealed spaces for shot glasses and small flasks and also places to store playing cards and poker chips; tall grandfather clocks that doubled as cocktail cabinets; and coffee tables with secret slide-in revolving sides for glasses, booze, and shakers were the rage both during Prohibition and after repeal.

Pla-Pal "Speakeasy" radio, Prohibition-era wooden radio with hidden bar, black enamel trim, and chrome, ca. 1928.

Open Pla-Pal radio revealing its hidden compartments.

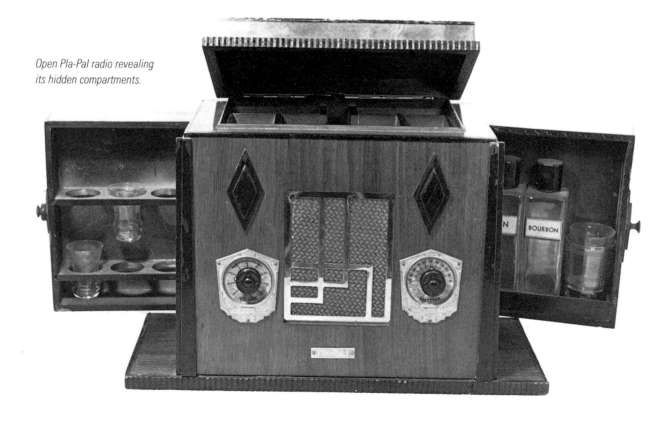

The Depression Kitchen

The typical American kitchen in the early years of the Depression was not so different from that of the 1920s and earlier. To be sure, there was more electrical gadgetry in the home: Waring Blendors, Sunbeam Mixmasters, automatic toasters, heavy chrome waffle irons, and monitor-top white-enamel refrigerators had replaced the icebox (no longer could father kid mother about mysterious interludes with the iceman). A gas range, if it was not black cast iron, was usually two-tone porcelain enamel, either marbleized black with white trim, tan with cream, or medium green with cream.

Initially kitchens were kept plain, painted cream, French blue, or Depression green (medium Nile-gray green) enamel. The all-purpose hutch or larder was also painted one of these colors and sometimes sported decal appliqués of tulips, Dutch girls, Dutch boys, windmills, and sailboats on its door panels. A hutch featured a porcelain-enamel work-counter, tin-lined drawers for bread and rolls, a flour bin; and often it came with enameled-tin cannister sets for coffee, tea, flour, sugar, and salt, with these names printed on them.

The kitchen table was usually painted pine with drop-leaf side panels and came with four matching chairs. Sanitary porcelain-enamel tables, often embellished with interesting varicolored geometric or floral Deco patterns, were also available.

Porcelain percolator with Catalin knob and chromium base and matching creamer and sugar container, Fraunfeiter China, Royal Rochester.

Late 1920s, early '30s kitchen in Depression green, with Art Deco–style linoleum, porcelain-enamel kitchen table-top and hutch, monitor-top refrigerator, free-standing stove and oven, Mixmaster, toaster, and assorted household products, from "Consumers Choice: The American Home 1890–1940," Delaware Art Museum, 1981.

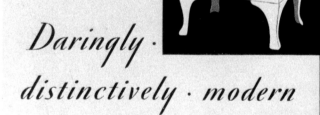

Daringly · distinctively · modern

TRUE to this dynamic age, when beauty is the unconscious outgrowth of the practical, the staunch lines of the General Electric reflect the spirit of modern art, thought, and architecture. Its distinctive design heralds a more advanced type of refrigeration service. In its Monitor Top is a simple modern mechanism, hushed in a blanket of oil—sealed, in a fortress of steel, against time and wear. Because this modern Refrigerator is so well-conceived and so ably constructed—and because it is so basically correct in contour—time blends it well into the setting of any kitchen. Its appearance literally grows on one. Like things we treasure most, it wears well, both mechanically and visually.

General Electric Company, Electric Refrigeration Department, Section B5, Hanna Building, 1400 Euclid Avenue, Cleveland, Ohio

GENERAL ⓖⓔ ELECTRIC
ALL-STEEL REFRIGERATOR
DOMESTIC, APARTMENT HOUSE, AND COMMERCIAL REFRIGERATORS, ELECTRIC WATER COOLERS

Join us in the General Electric Program, broadcast every Saturday evening, on a nation-wide N. B. C. network

Woolworth's and other dime stores like S. H. Kress, H. L. Green, McCrory's, and S. S. Kresge sold transparent glass dinnerware that became ubiquitous in 1930s kitchens. Cheaply priced, it was called Depression-ware, Depression glass, or "Tank" glass. Tinted in cobalt blue, pink (or peach), yellow, red, amber, and light, medium, or dark green, the glassware also came in "plain-clear." Initially the most produced, light and medium green are the most common colors found today at flea markets and in antique shops. Many intricate design patterns were used, and often Art Deco fountains, skyscraper motifs, pyramid triangles, zigzags, or a moderne pattern of parallel lines were embossed on this glass. Opaque Jadite green, Delphite blue, and black and white "milk" glass also fit into the Depression-ware category. Thick Jadite green ware was especially popular for restaurants, cafeterias, or diners in the 1930s. Whether it was salt and pepper shakers, measuring cups, water pitchers, a flower vase, refrigerator jars, or cake

21-PIECE COLORED GLASS
Luncheon Set
Yours FOR ONLY
59¢
CASH PRICE
WITH THE FIRST ORDER OF A NEW CLUB!

For full details see preceding page

plates, Depression-ware turned up in almost every home, with a great number of glass companies like Hazel Atlas, Heisey, Hocking, McKee and Jeannette competing in this vast marketplace. Housewives would often build their dish sets by going once a week to the Rex, Rialto, or Ritz on "Dish-nite" to see a double-feature movie, previews of coming attractions, shorts, and a Mickey Mouse cartoon. Here they happily accepted a cup, saucer, gravy boat, or creamer from the manager who greeted them with a smile.

Ashtrays made of Depression green glass were used throughout the house, and at the bar father might mix a drink from a translucent red, cobalt blue, or green glass decanter or cocktail shaker. Depression glass, more than any other single item, always evokes the Deco period and is today collected by thousands of people who belong to special Depression glass clubs and subscribe to newspapers like *Depression Daze*, whose readers through its ads trade and sell their dishes by mail. When seen stacked in a china closet at home or on window shelves in a shop, the sun streaming through, this glass is very colorful and cheerful.

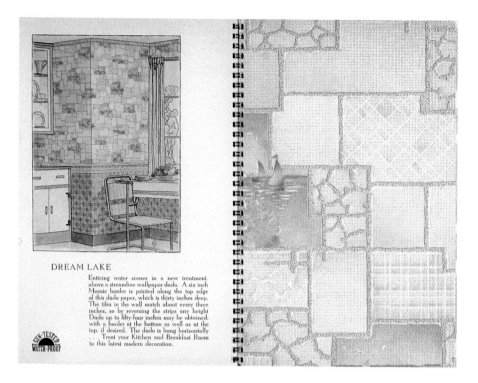

Illustration featuring kitchen setting and modern "sun-tested" and waterproofed wallpaper from Tribune Wallpaper Company booklet, Elizabeth, New Jersey, 1930s.

Depression-green glass salt and pepper shakers with a geometric Deco pattern and red Bakelite tops are set in a glass "boat."

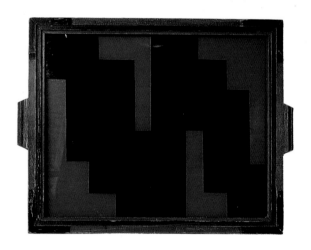

Painted wood and painted-on-reverse glass serving tray in Depression green and black, in zigzag skyscraper Deco style, ca. 1935.

The streamlined Sunbeam Automatic Mixmaster is an attractive electric kitchen appliance that came with three different-size Depression-green "Jadite" glass mixing bowls with a juicer attachment, ca. 1935.

The Streamlined Kitchen

Industrial designers and new manufacturers in the Depression era began to convince mother and dad that they should totally remodel their kitchen in Streamline Moderne with built-in efficiency units and cabinets, Monel metal sinks, and all-white enamel stoves and refrigerators, all promising a more sanitary and "scientific" environment in which to store, prepare, and eat food. In household magazines of the day, inviting advertisements for a modern kitchen read, "Come In. It's Fun to Work Here!" or "Modernize Your Comforts and Economize Your Cares!"

The "all-electric" kitchen was updated yearly by newly designed aerodynamic, streamline-style "pop-up" toasters and coffee urns, electric mixers, food-steaming trays, kitchen clocks, and even small countertop radios. "Fridgedaires," washing machines, and stoves began to look more modernistic with each year's latest model. In 1933 ads proclaimed "A Complete New Deal for the Forgotten Kitchen," heralding a Norman Bel Geddes–designed white porcelain-enameled stove. Housewives who longed for an easy-to-clean gas-range unit finally had a major kitchen appliance in sanitary white, refashioned with "skirts" to the floor, panels to cover burners, and other modern, eye-pleasing, labor-saving features. The stoves were sold by dealers as "Innovations in Design," and each one bore the designer's monogram. In effect,

these stoves can be thought of, by today's standards, as "signed" artist's pieces. The Coldspot refrigerator, introduced in 1934 and designed by Raymond Loewy for Sears, superseded the monitor-top refrigerator and added the final touch to the new, modern look for the streamlined kitchen.

Recessed Lumalite lighting was recommended for the kitchen with the idea that lighting should be bright, yet indirect and never harsh. Paper or canvas window shades were replaced by metal venetian blinds that came in bright new kitchen colors, and sometimes glass brick was added in appropriate areas for a dramatic effect. Dishware cabinets that once were open or with wood-frame glass doors now kept all utensils, products, and dishes hidden from view behind solid panels.

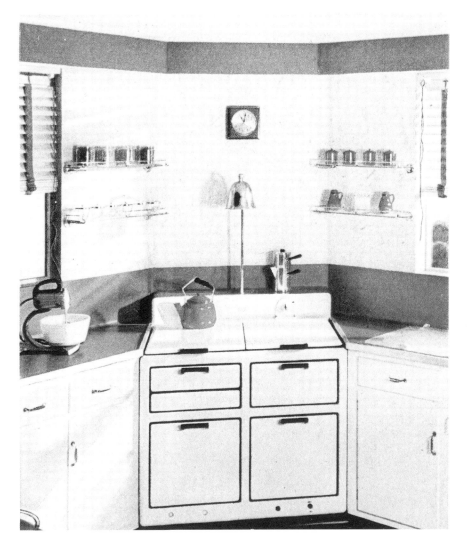

The revolutionary modern refrigerator designed by Raymond Loewy for Coldspot boosted sales from 15,000 units to 275,000 within five years.

Opposite: "The nation walks on Pabco floors," four-color, geometric, inlaid kitchen linoleum manufactured by Paraffine Co., Inc.

Cherry red and marble white linoleum kitchen from Sealex Wall Linoleum booklet, 1937.

Streamlined "American Beauty" iron with colored Lucite and black Bakelite handle, manufactured by the American Electrical Heater Co., Detroit, Michigan, ca. 1940.

Am *I* the Lucky Girl!

'JUST WHAT I WANTED' DOESN'T HALF EXPRESS IT!

"The minute I laid eyes on these good-looking Universal gifts, I knew what I wanted. They'll help me so with entertaining and housekeeping. And I know they'll serve for a long time to come. Mother says anything Universal *must* be good. That's one trademark which was a household word when she too, was young."

5 SMART NEW MEMBERS OF A FAMOUS FAMILY

TURN-EASY TOASTER—second to none in styling. Pattern is "Coronet"—newest and smartest. Mirror-bright chromium finish. All trimmings of ever-cool, black bakelite. The price is news, too. $3.95

NEW "GLIDER"—unique among irons. Air-cooled, protects hands from heat radiation. Other features include: lightweight, fingertip control, beveled point, a wrinkle-proof round heel. Price $7.95

WAFFLE MAKER in "Coronet" pattern. Built close to table for easier serving. Soft light signals when to pour batter, when to serve. Heat control assures waffles as you like them. $8.95

ONLY THE UNIVERSAL Food Mixer gives full power at every speed. New direct drive does away with costly extra power unit. Multi-speed control, 3- and 1-quart glass bowls. $21.00

NEW MIXABLEND—(*extreme right*). One appliance that's never on the shelf. Whips, beats, mixes, chops. Adds new health foods and drinks to your menu. Amazingly powerful. Complete in itself. $19.95

UNIVERSAL
THE TRADE MARK KNOWN IN EVERY HOME

Smart giving starts at your Universal dealer's. See him today for practical gift suggestions

LANDERS, FRARY & CLARK
New Britain, Connecticut

This modern kitchen included a breakfast nook with chrome-leatherette chairs, venetian blinds, and the latest in kitchen floor linoleum. Sealex Wall Linoleum booklet, 1937.

Kitchen appliances of the 1930s depicted in this ad from Landers, Frary and Clark of New Britain, Connecticut, include chromium waffle maker, "Turn-easy" toaster, "Universal" food mixer, "Mix-a-blend" blender, and "glider" iron, all featuring "Ever-cool" black Bakelite, from House Beautiful, November 1940.

Modern kitchen china made in Japan and sold at F. W. Woolworth's in the 1930s, available in blue or sepia tones; Moderne chromium coffee percolator patented in 1922; "Turnover" toaster with Art Deco fountain motif, Westinghouse Electric Mfg. Co., ca. 1927; half-pint "Baby Face" milk bottle, "For Mothers Who Care," Brookfield Dairy, Hellertown, Pennsylvania, 1930s.

Modern work-saving kitchen with Monel metal sink, steel furniture with baked-enamel finish, exhibited at the Town of Tomorrow and the Home Building Center at the New York World's Fair of 1939. Whitehead Metal Products Co., New York, brochure illustrated by Schroyer, 1937.

Five-piece chromium coffee set from Sunbeam Co., including coffee pot, electric warming unit, creamer, sugar container, and serving tray.

*Geometric Deco-patterned
kitchen linoleum, ca. 1930s.*

*Magic-Maid Automatic
Toaster with skyscraper and
floral Deco pattern, Fitzgerald
Manufacturing Co., Torrington,
Connecticut, 1934.*

The porcelain-enamel tabletop with Bauhaus-type patterns embossed on it had tubular chrome legs with matched "leatherette"-and-chrome chairs replacing the "old-fashioned" painted wooden kitchen sets.

Sets of Catalin or other brand-name plastic-handled knives, forks, and spoons added modish Deco accents to these kitchens; one or two corresponding colors like red or cream were employed to blend into a kitchen color scheme. A streamlined kitchen, for the first time, used such bright paint colors as red, yellow, or royal blue with matched contrasts of softer browns, gray, green, or a strong navy blue or black. Linoleum was incorporated into these kitchen color plans, using bold geometric patterns or sweeping-swirling runs of color that often would end in a circle in the center of the room.

In 1939 Russel Wright created the most stream-lined and modernistic dish sets when he designed "American Modern" dinnerware for Steubenville in an array of muted colors, including chartreuse, granite gray, seafoam, canteloupe, cedar green, coral, white, bean brown, glacier, and black chutney. The "coupe" shapes and speckled glazes represented a cross between streamlining and Surrealism and brought a new added symbol of progress from an important industrial designer to the ultramodern kitchen. In the early 1930s Wright designed spun aluminum home accessories with clean, sharp beauty for a number of companies. These pieces included a samovar, coffee pots, a tea set, ice pails, beer pitchers, and other elegant moderne pieces. He also designed items in chrome for the Chase Brass and Copper Company, which regularly employed the best industrial designers for its lines of chrome and copper objects and home accessories.

Product manufacturers kept apace with the "design decade" by offering boldly modernistic and colorful packaging to fit into the new scheme of the modern kitchen. Detergent boxes, scouring-cleanser cans, coffee tins, Log Cabin Syrup tins, and other consumer products all had to compete in this new marketplace.

In the April 1935 issue of *Arts and Decoration*, the editors scolded "new-fangled" designers with the admonition that "the kitchen is the one scientific room in most houses and it should look both work-manlike and spotless. But there is no need for it to look like a laboratory, while so many industrial designers hug the 'woman's part of the house' to their hearts." In a 1936 *Arts and Decoration*, Walter Dorwin Teague replied, "Painting and sculpture are art but so is the making of kitchen sinks and pickle bottles."

Industrial designers like Mr. Teague did not miss a (breakfast) nook or (corner cabinet) cranny in their desire to make over the world of the kitchen—and everything else along with it.

American Modern teapot designed in 1937 by Russel Wright.

Deco Mexicana

Housewives in the Depression could not avoid collecting kitchen bric-a-brac or utilitarian artifacts, be they glass or metal cannister sets, streamlined tin breadboxes with Catalin knobs, or humorous figural ceramic cookie jars like the ones featuring southern mammies. One thing was certain in the 1930s: south-of-the-border-down-Mexico-way motifs for use in the kitchen were all the rage. The bright, intense colors of old Mexico fit into the new modern schemes of remodeled kitchens and also seemed to lift the gray spirit of "Old Man Depression," who many felt was about to be ousted, any day, by "Kid Prosperity." Just as Art Deco had originally used flowers, fountains, and ferns over pure geometric line, so the colorful "Mexicana" theme came into play in the streamlined American kitchen.

Wall decorations, knickknack figurines, planters, salt and pepper shakers, curtains, dishtowels, embroidered napkins and napkin holders, brightly patterned tablecloths, drink sets, and dish sets all featured various images of colorful Mexican pottery: senoritas dancing amidst flowers and palms, hombres in oversize sombreros taking a "siesta" in the sun next to giant cacti or mules, or market vendors holding up bowls of sun-ripened vegetables and fruit. Life in Mexico appeared to be simple, warm, and without care, and Mexicana images lent an air of relaxation to a kitchen setting.

Framed embroidered Mexicana-style kitchen wall decoratives, handmade by Olga Heitke, ca. 1938.

Painted-on-reverse glass and wood-framed Deco Mexicana-style kitchen snack trays, ca. 1940.

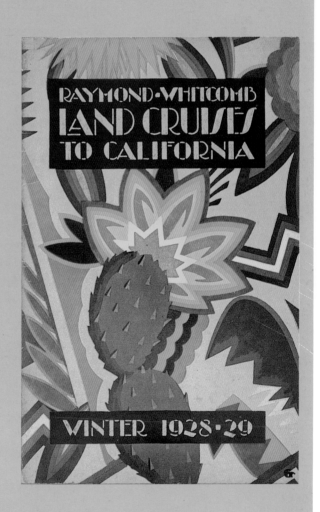

Winter 1928–29 Land Cruise travel booklet, featuring Art Deco cover illustrations of California desert cactus and flowers. Raymond and Whitcomb Company of Chicago.

Kitchen shelves featuring
Caliente dinnerware (marked
Shell-Krest) in the Deco
apartment of Jeffrey Geiger
and Tim Goetz in Manhattan.
Produced by Paden City Pot-
tery Company, Paden City,
West Virginia, ca. 1930s.

Deco Dishes

The J. A. Bauer Pottery Company was among the first to bring "hot" colors into the kitchens of southern California, where the company originated and where many homes were built in the Adobe-Hacienda or Mission style, which employed cement-stucco on the entire facade, ceramic pipe roofing, and Spanish tile and wrought-iron detailing. In the midst of the retail market's Depression gloom in 1930, Bauer produced sets of multicolor dishware in a spectrum of highly glazed colors, including Jade green, Delph blue (light), Royal blue (dark), black, Chinese yellow, and a California orange-red. The intense red was made with uranium, which had to be imported from the Belgian Congo (now Zaire).

So popular was Bauer's California-colored pottery—in design lines called La Linda, El Chico, and Monterrey Moderne—which included varied "technicolor" nesting bowls, large urns and oil jars, and other utilitarian pieces in addition to their regular dishware, that other pottery firms rapidly followed suit. California residents or tourists could now bring home "souvenir pottery" for their Hacienda-style kitchens from the popular vacation resort of Catalina Island where the first colored pottery was manufactured. Under the name Catalina Clay Products, a solid-color dishware was marketed as "Avalonware."

Fiesta-ware "Red" coffeepot made by the Homer-Laughlin China Co. (Mood Indigo, Soho, New York City)

Harlequin coffee cup on a special combination saucer/ashtray available in 1938 from the Homer Laughlin China Co. and sold at F. W. Woolworth's. Also shown is a teaspoon with a red Catalin handle, a Lucky Strike Green cigarette pack, and a Horn and Hardart Company souvenir matchbook welcoming World's Fair visitors to Manhattan in 1939.

The "Big Five" manufacturers of this type of pottery were J. A. Bauer; Gladding McBean & Co., which featured a Franciscan-ware and an El Patio line; the Pacific Clay Products Company, which began producing a line in bright shades called "Hostess-ware" in 1932; Vernon Kilns, which started making "art pottery" in 1916 and entered the colored-pottery field with a line called "Montecito"; and the Metlox Poppy Trail Manufacturing Company. Other "Mexican-design" companies that created interesting dishware were the American Ceramic Company, with "La Mirada"; the Santa Anita Potteries; Caliente; Yorktowne, with a "Mango" red; and Meyers, with its "California Rainbow."

One of the first companies in the East to notice this colorful and lucrative dishware trend was the Homer-Laughlin China Company of Newell, West Virginia, which introduced its phenomenally successful Fiesta-ware in 1936. A Fiesta-ware ad in that year declared, "Originating in California, inspired by the colorful spectacles of Mexico, Fiesta Dinnerware has flashed across the country in a gay blaze of color. Its beautiful rainbow shades have captivated the hearts of housewives, bringing cheer and gayety into the home, adding festive charm to al fresco dining."

Designed by an Englishman named Frederick Rhead, Fiesta dishes featured an original color roster of dark cobalt, turquoise, medium green, old ivory, yellow, and a brilliant Fiesta orange-red. Later colors included rose, gray, forest green, and chartreuse. The Homer-Laughlin Company, which had wide distribution in department stores all over the country, replaced their antiquated dipping tubs with high-speed conveyor belts and an automated spray-glazing machine that could handle 30,000 pieces of Fiesta per day.

Meanwhile, at the dime store, mother could buy "Harlequin," a cheaper pottery that also featured bright colors. This was sold exclusively at Woolworth's. A line called "Tango" was sold at J. J. Newberry. These brands, including one called "Riviera," were all produced by the Homer-Laughlin Company and today sell at smart Deco shops for high prices, right alongside the quality Fiesta-ware or Bauer. In the late 1930s a complete seventy-six-piece set of Fiesta Dinnerware sold for $20 or less, depending on the outlet. Large salad bowls, juice pitchers, coffee pots, wine carafes, compotes, syrup dispensers, bud or full-size flower vases, candle holders, mustard pots, covered casserole dishes, and marmalade jars cost extra. They are, by the same standard, high-price collector's pieces due to their rarity. A Fiesta syrup pitcher, for example, might cost $100 today. As well as glazed ceramic tumblers in all colors, Fiesta also produced clear glass tumblers embossed with colorful Mexican sombreros, cacti, water jugs, and other bright symbols of Mexican life.

Fiesta gravy boat designed by Frederick Rhead for Homer-Laughlin China Co.

Another line of Fiesta-ware was called Kitchen Kraft, decorated with striking "Mexicana," Indian, and sunflower patterns. Kitchen Kraft also had a separate line in solid colors of red, blue, yellow, and green. Large platters, casseroles, mixing bowls, pie plates, covered jugs and jars, and sturdy-looking bulbous-shaped salt and pepper shakers for the kitchen range were a highlight of the popular Kitchen Kraft sets, which featured underglaze Mexican-inspired decal images on an ivory cream-colored body. In the gay spirit of old Mexico, decal appliqués were sold everywhere in America in the 1930s, including the hardware store, the five-and-dime store, and novelty and variety stores. These were transferred onto glassware and kitchen cabinets with decorative abandon.

The use of South-of-the-Border decor continued on into the 1940s, when the United States developed its "friendly neighbor" policy, but Fiesta red "went to war" along with Lucky Strike green and cobalt blue. The "cobalt" that was an ingredient in manufacturing atomic bombs had been used in blue Depressionware dishes and blue mirrors. Eliminating the solid green on Lucky Strike cigarette packaging was said to have aided the war effort by saving bronze (the new red, black, and white package was designed by Raymond Loewy), and certain elements that went into producing Fiesta red could not be imported during wartime.

"Aladdin Lamp" streamlined teapot, gloss pastel kitchenware manufactured by J. A. Bauer Pottery Co., Los Angeles, California, 1941.

Kitchen Kraft meat platter with Mexicana pattern in the Fiesta-ware line of dishware, from Homer Laughlin China Co., ca. 1939.

Frankart Nude Nymphets

During the first three decades of this century, Broadway musicals, Hollywood films, and exotic musical revues "glorified" the American girl, adorning her in expensive furs, plumes, and jewels. Stage stars of the day like Marilyn Miller, Ruth Etting, or the Dolly Sisters were presented by showmen George White or Florenz Ziegfeld as goddesslike images of feminine perfection. Many of the shows featured nudity, often in the guise of a "living" tableau of beautiful women, some draped seductively in sheer transparent fabric.

Much of the fine Art Deco bronze/ivory statuary of D. Chiparus, F. Preiss, Alonzo, Jacquemin, Bruno Zack, and other artisans was inspired by showgirls in the *Ziegfeld Follies* and the Casino de Paris, or by cabaret dancer-singers like Josephine Baker, a ravishing black American who created a stir in Paris in the twenties when she appeared, often nude, singing her jazzy, sophisticated songs.

Dancing-lady nude statuettes for use as decorative objects in the parlor, bar, or den came to symbolize a new liberated attitude toward sensuality in the emerging modernist age. Leading the way was French sculptor Max Le Verrier who created highly stylized nude figurines of women with modernelike features and streamlined hairstyles. Cast in white metal and finished in a green patina that was meant to simulate aged copper or bronze, these "green ladies," as they were called in the twenties, stood on tiered black-marble bases with outstretched hands holding up electric lights in frosted globes. Mood-lamp green-lady statuettes became conversation pieces that gave a touch of outré to home decor in the twenties and thirties, and they have come to be thought of as a primary object-form that symbolizes the Art Deco era. Sold originally in Paris at the prestigious art/gift salon Primavera, Le Verrier pieces, including bookend sets and lamps, were exported for sale in the United States. These became prototypes for American manufacturers' own mass-produced versions—sold for prices that would attract the middle-class consumer.

Art Deco mood lamp on a blue mirror by Le Verrier, painted in green finish on French metal and set on marble base. Sold originally at Primavera in Paris, 1925.

placques, vase holders, candle sets, cigarette stands (with glass containers), fishbowl stands, fruit bowls, candy dishes, and the like were sold at better department stores, gift shops, or through sales catalogs. Most popular were the "mood lamps" that featured

Diana the Huntress, stylized Deco wall plaque in chromium, stamped Frankart, Inc., 1930.

Green painted metal twin-nude-nymphet cigarette holder with glass box insert, Frankart, Inc.

The most prominent and prolific of the small manufacturing firms that produced such design pieces was Frankart, Inc., which styled itself as "manufacturers of objects of Art in metal." The main salesroom and offices of the company were located at 225 Fifth Avenue, a design studio was at 33 West 67th Street, and a factory at 542-548 Casanova Street, all in Manhattan. Arthur von Frankenberg, the zealous president of the company who was also its art director, sculpted his various nude statuettes himself from live models, preferably women with long, lithe bodies and angular features.

Frankart, Inc.'s first "nudie" was produced in 1921. Called "Flame," it was a candle holder in the Art Nouveau style. Following the opening of King Tut's tomb in 1922 and the rage for anything Egyptian, von Frankenberg added stepped-up tiers to his statuary bases, introducing a more Deco style. Imprinted "Frankart, Inc." on the base, along with a date and a patent number, these nude statuettes, bookend sets, floor-standing or table ashtrays, clocks, wall masks,

Metal and glass flower vase, Frankart, Inc., 1928.

Mood lamp in white metal painted Depression green with nudes gazing into green glass-rod fixture, marked Frankart, 1927.

Standing ashtray with gold copper finish, Frankart, Inc.

one, two, or more nude figures staring into a light, holding a large crackle-glass globe up into the air, or sitting in front of a glass cylinder meant to diffuse the light and create a dramatic effect. Silhouette mood lamps usually had a single nude holding up a round piece of frosted or rippled glass in front of a light or positioned in front of a rectangular, tinted glass. Also called "shadow lamps," these exotic artifacts became status symbols in homes and apartments, often placed on a fireplace mantel, an end table, a bedroom vanity, or a hall console. In this early period of modernity there was a mystical fascination with electric light, and these novelty lamps were an aspect of

attempting to use "Mazda-lite" in colorful, new, and interesting ways. Shadow or mood lamps were also placed on round blue mirrors in order to reflect light.

All Frankart products were cast metal, aluminum alloy, Brittania, or French metal. A 1930–31 Frankart, Inc., catalog refers to "bronze finishes" on these statuettes, but in reality they were painted in the following colors: Jap (a very dark brown with green crevices), Depression green (a medium Nile-gray green), dark green with light-green speckles, gunmetal gray, black ebony, copper gold, or luminescent ivory. The most popular color for the Frankart line was Depression green. Crackle-glass globes or cylinders were

available in a number of frosted colors, including rose, green, amber, crystal, and white.

If you study Busby Berkeley's *Gold Diggers of 1933*, *Footlight Parade*, or *Dames* closely, you will spot Frankarts sitting on coffee tables or nightstands in Joan Blondell's or Ruby Keeler's New York apartments. They may also be noted in Marx Brothers' movies.

Arthur von Frankenberg imbued these unique pieces with the same elfin, gamine quality seen in the androgynous men and women of the popular paintings, prints, and calendars of Maxfield Parrish. Other 1930s companies imitated the Frankart line, but the products made by Nu-Art and Eckart do not have the anatomical perfection and "esprit" of Mr. von Frankenberg's figurines.

Frankart, Inc., also added comical cowgirls, cowboys, gauchos, street cleaners, hunters, waiters, golfers, babies, Herculean men, and other characters to their specialty line; many of the "funny" pieces were designed for the firm by John Held, Jr., one of the foremost caricaturists to come out of the roaring twenties. Monkeys, seals, leaping deer, ibex, wolves, dogs, elephants, bear cubs, and puffed-up doves were also part of the Frankart line. It is the nude-nymphet statuary, however, created as useful and functional pieces for the home, that have come to be among the most prized Art Deco collector pieces today.

Many of these are reproduced for today's "Echo Deco" marketplace, but the newer versions are often crudely painted, without attention to detail, and, wisely, are not imprinted with the original Frankart signature.

Frankart, Inc., went out of business in the Depression, and in the mid-1940s most of the original von Frankenberg molds were, unfortunately, sold by weight as scrap metal and destroyed.

An original Frankart catalog reads, "Particular em-

Opposite:
Two Egyptian-style nude-nymphets holding up crackle-glass globe. Electric lamp, height 18 in., made by Frankart, Inc., 1928.

Nude-nymphet "shadow lamp" holding circular rippled-glass "moon," height 16 in., Frankart, Inc., 1930.

Combination ashtray and cigarette box in green milk glass with stylized painted nude, marked Frankart, ca. 1930.

Gunmetal gray Frankart figures holding copper fruit bowl aloft, 1928.

Monkey ash receiver, Frankart, Inc., catalog, 1931.

Puffed-up dove, gold patina ashtray, Frankart, Inc., 1927.

Leaping gazelle bookend, gunmetal finish on white metal, Frankart, Inc., 1927.

phasis has been stressed on artistic conceptions of streamline designs expressing the modern vogue. Inventive ingenuity has happily combined with artistic ability to create objets d'art of practicability."

Though many of these individually molded objects that were mass produced in Frankart's small New York factory (there were over 150 different variations) now sell for hundreds of dollars, the original prices, as seen in a 1933 L & C Mayers Company Merchandise Catalogue, were in a range of $4 to $20, with nudie bookends selling for $4, a dinner gong for $7, a shadow lamp for $13.50, and a beautiful smoking stand for $14.

Puttin' on the Dog

Deco-period dogs that appear on graphics, in magazine advertisements, vintage greeting cards, on drinking glass tumblers and pitchers, decks of bridge and pinochle playing cards, on ashtrays, and as decorative statuary for the 1930s living room or office number many of the most-esteemed terriers, including the Scottish, the Boston, the fox, the Kerry blue, and the wire-haired, in addition to the borzoi, the whippet, and the greyhound.

In the 1920s German shepherds enjoyed a great popularity, inspired by the famous movie dogs Strongheart and Rin Tin Tin, and many objects such as ashtrays, incense burners, and mood lamps from the twenties featured a shepherd.

In the 1930s glamorous ladies of the stage and screen took to walking the elegant borzoi, greyhound, and whippet, which in terms of streamlining and as symbols of speed were very appealing to moderne tastes. Images of these dogs appeared frequently on jewelry, in Louis Icart prints, and, of course, a running greyhound became the trademark symbol of a renowned bus company.

Boston terriers, then called Boston bull terriers, are almost synonymous with the 1920s and '30s, when they enjoyed their greatest popularity as the first American purebred dog. Betty Boop's black-and-white rascal sidekick Bimbo, with his bulging Eddie Cantor banjo eyes, is a Boston terrier, a lively "out-of-the-

Congress playing cards featuring the elegant and graceful borzoi, 1930s.

Boston terrier Depression-era cast-iron doorstop.

The Dog Bar matchbook claimed on the inside cover that it was ''America's only Dog Bar.'' The ''canine'' bar for humans was in the Hotel West Falls, West Falls, New York (18 miles from downtown Buffalo).

Fala, the famous White House ''Scottie'' whose master was the equally famous Franklin Delano Roosevelt, had his own 78rpm record album on Monarch Records, Inc. His name and image also appeared on schoolbook readers, storybooks, coloring books, and pencil boxes throughout the 1930s and '40s. A comic Fala is seen here making mischief on the White House lawn.

''Hoot Mon'' Scottie dog playing card set came in an attractive box from Russell Playing Card Co., New York, 1932.

Catalin novelty Scottie costume-jewelry dress pin, carved and hand-painted with glass eye insert.

Boston bull terrier Art Deco–design playing card, 1930.

Playing card featuring wire-haired terrier and Scottish terrier, both popular canines of the 1930s and '40s.

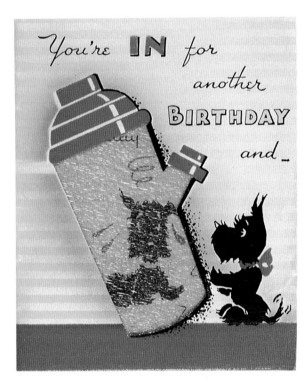

Comic birthday-greeting card featuring the ubiquitous black Scottie, shown here with cocktail shaker. Inside a very drunk dog is shown with the sentiment, ''Speaking of 'good shakers' I'd like to shake your hand while wishing you a jolly 'mix' of birthday pleasures grand!''

Black, white, and red Scotties cavort on glass kitchen tumbler.

Boston terrier featured on the cover of Nature *magazine,* November 1931, *in an infinity repeat image.*

inkwell" creation of cartoonist Max Fleischer. The Boston terrier image turns up frequently as painted iron doorstops, which were ubiquitous items in the 1930s household, as incense burners (incense burned in the dog's mouth came out as smoke through its nostrils), on Frankart ashtrays, and on bridge score-cards, playing cards, glass knickknacks, and many other decorative and amusing household items.

The wire-haired terrier is also represented on a variety of similar objects due to the fame of an M-G-M dog star named Asta, who helped elegant William Powell and sophisticated Myrna Loy, as the Dashiell Hammett detective couple, solve their cases in *The Thin Man* film series.

Outdoing all of these dogs in 1930s fashion was President Roosevelt's beloved companion, the Scottie Fala. Not only were there books and coloring books for children telling the story of the president's dog, but the Scottie, wearing a plaid or red collar, was utilized with great frequency on everything from dish-towels to napkins and on pillows, glasses, serving trays, bowls, canisters, pincushions, planters, or as decorative glass or metal statuary. The Fala fad reached great heights in the thirties, and once again, in this Deco-revival period, Scotties have become fashion-able and are winning top honors at dog shows.

Scottish terriers on hand-embroidered plaid napkin; red Catalin napkin holder, yellow Catalin baby spoon, green and cream plastic children's utensils.

Just as cats today are seen everywhere, on every conceivable kind of merchandise, on calendars, and as subjects for books, in the Depression era it was the well-bred dog that had his day.

Other animals and critters found as elements or symbols in Art Deco design are the polar bear, the seal, and the penguin, made instantly popular world-wide after Admiral Byrd's trip to the South Pole. Other prominent subjects within the Deco canon were the eagle, falcon, puffed-up dove, turkey, and pigeon. Camels, horses, elephants, foxes, wild boar, bison, panthers, and lions also appeared within the context of Deco decorative schemes. Leaping gazelles, ante-lopes, and the theme of *les biches* recur again and again in the twenties and thirties on everything from fine glassware to statuary, clocks, and other objects, or as ornamentation on divider screens and architec-tural bronze grillwork.

Red plastic Scottie dog dress pin with moving head, 1930s.

RADIO AGE

Wide-scale manufacturing of radio sets began in 1920, but it was not until 1927, with "A-C plug-ins," that the radio became a permanent fixture in the American home. The earliest forms of radio, with roots going back as far as 1887, were the wireless and the crystal sets with their cumbersome cornucopia speakers and complex paraphernalia. These kept radio in the hobbyist or experimental stage for some time, but by 1928, when factories were producing 75,000 sets each week for shipment to music stores, department stores, and furniture outlets, radio had come of age.

In 1933, in the midst of the Great Depression, 26 million Americans owned a radio purchased at an average cost of $100. By 1938 a family could buy an eight-tube, automatic "touch-tune" console model with improved "hardware" created to "house" the set and speaker for $49.95, but by then the popular "Baby" table model could be bought in the $9.95 category at many salesrooms.

Radio had a tremendous impact on the average citizen, breaking down barriers of regionalism, narrowing the gap between city and country, and opening up a new age of information and entertainment for the entire world. While not everyone went to "the pictures," no one could escape "the great synthesizer" that had entered their very own living room. With radio signals burning nightly through the ether, mother, father, sister, junior, and the family dog Rex would gather together in the parlor to listen, dream, and enter into the magic auditory dimension of "sound." Radio appealed to the imagination and could stimulate "pictures" in the mind of the listener—no matter that crumpling cellophane in front of a microphone produced the sound of a crackling fire or that coconut shells hitting a soundboard mimicked the galloping hoofbeats of the great horse Silver, the Lone Ranger's white stallion.

Radio's mass appeal revolutionized the advertising

Classic, aerodynamic teardrop, butterscotch Catalin table-model Fada "Streamliner" radio, manufactured in 1941 by Fada Radio & Electric. Co., Inc., Long Island City, New York.

Kate Smith Memories Song Book *compiled by Kate Smith for Robbins Music Corp., New York.*

Decorative endpaper illustra-tion for All About Amos 'n' Andy and Their Creators Correll and Gosden, *published by Rand McNally & Co., 1929.*

Tabletop ebony-black plastic radio sold originally in 1940 for $9.25 from Allied Radio catalog, Chicago, Illinois.

Matchbook advertising a brown Bakelite Crosley table-model radio.

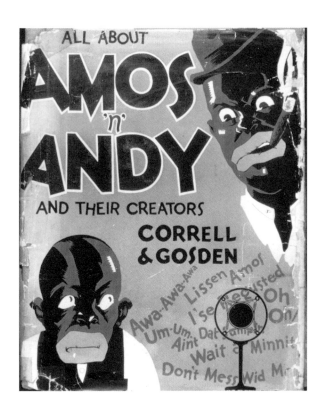

was at least one radio in each American home and one in every car.

The most popular radio set for the home was an imposing four-legged console that housed six, eight, or more large tubes, a speaker, a tuning dial, control knobs, and, sometimes, the added feature of a 78 rpm phonograph hidden in a sliding compartment. These handsomely crafted pieces of furniture became the focal point for the living room then just as a television set often is today.

As a status symbol, the 1929 family might purchase a finely constructed, gleaming hardwood, eight-tube Stromberg-Carlson console (the Packard of radios) for $380 while the powerful RCA Radiola specialty console was $575. Radio sets came down considerably in price during the Depression years, with most house-

All About Amos 'n' Andy and Their Creators Correll & Gosden, book with dust jacket by C. J. Correll (Andy) and F. F. Gosden (Amos), published by Rand McNally & Co., copyright 1929.

Charlie McCarthy Majestic radio in white enamel on metal with the figurine in painted metal alloy, 1938.

medium, and news reports, broadcast live, could now be heard around the clock. Sports, prizefights, political conventions, and FDR, who first instituted his Fireside Chats from the White House on March 12, 1933, could rivet listeners to their radios, giving them the impression that they were right there at the event. By the 1930s, tuning in to your favorite programs—"Amos 'n' Andy" (the most popular, with 30 million weekly listeners), based on two black characters from Harlem played by two white former vaudevillians Freeman Gosden and Charles Correll; "Fibber McGee and Molly," which holds the record for the second all-time highest rating for a radio program; "One Man's Family, and His Bewildering Offspring"; or "The Kate Smith Show," featuring the Songbird of the South —had become a steady radio routine. By 1940 there

"Radio Orphan Annie's 1939 Official Secret Society Membership Manual" contains secret passwords, ads for sending away for Orphan Annie decoder pins and other Ovaltine radio premium giveaways. This page from the booklet illustrates Annie and her Harold Gray comic-strip pals coming to life right out of the family radio set. Published by the Wander Co. of Chicago, Illinois—makers of Ovaltine.

Emerson superheterodyne radio on an advertising matchbook.

IT'S ORPHAN ANNIE TIME!

DON'T MISS IT!

MEET us in front of your radio every day at Orphan Annie time! Listen to Annie's adventures on the radio—every single day except Saturday and Sunday. And be sure you're on time, so you won't miss anything!

You never can tell when Orphan Annie may be broadcasting an *important secret message* in the new 1939 mystery code that's explained on page 6 of this book! There'll be lots of secret messages that no one but 1939 members can understand! So always have a pencil and paper with you at the radio ready to take down messages! And listen *every night*— so you'll be right up-to-date on Annie's thrilling new adventures!

holds buying on the installment plan, $5 down and $5 per month. While Atwater-Kent, Stromberg-Carlson, and Sparton sets were in the more expensive category, the most common were from RCA, Philco, Zenith, and Silvertone's all-wave "Wonder Radio," which sold through the Sears catalogs. Zenith introduced moderne styling for their deluxe console cabinetware and featured a white lightning-bolt dial against a black background on which were printed call letters of distant radio stations coast to coast. Zenith was famous for the magic "green eye" that glowed mysteriously when the tubes warmed up.

The technology of radio had improved by the mid-1930s, and so had radio hardware. Industrial designers were hired by radio companies to take their cabinets from Rosebud–Gothic cathedral or Ginger-bread rococo styling into the sleeker contours of Streamline Moderne. The aerodynamic teardrop superheterodyne "Baby" Fada table radio, with a machine-molded, polished Catalin cabinet, is a first-rate example of how designers changed the shape of the smaller units. The modernistic styling has one side squared off and the other curved, as in the streamlining of automobiles like the Chrysler and DeSoto Airflows. Despite the fact that Frank A. D'Andrea sold the rights to his Long Island City company in 1934, the Fada "bullets," as they were called on the assembly line, continued to be produced until just after the war.

The Sparks-Withington Company, producer of Sparton radios, hired Walter Dorwin Teague to design several models, which resembled automobile grilles and dashboards. Teague combined cobalt blue, peach, or green

Radio Mirror *magazine, June 1935, cover portrait of the lovely singer Ruth Etting, sometimes billed as "Chicago's Sweetheart" and also called "The Glamorous Vocal Garbo," by famed illustrator A. Mozert.*

Radio Mirror *magazine, October 1934, featuring the dynamic "Songbird of the South," Miss Kate Smith, who had one of the top radio shows.*

Zenith Stratosphere Console twenty-five-tube radio with three concert speakers and split-second timing, in ebonized finish or conventional walnut, Fortune *magazine,* November 1938.

Streamlined Sparton radio in metal with imitation wood-grain lithography, designed by Walter Dorwin Teague to resemble an automobile dashboard, Sparks-Withington Co., 1935.

Aerodynamic, lipstick-red Plexon and Lucite table radio, Cyart Manufacturing Company, ca. 1946.

Cathedral-style yellow Catalin Emerson radio, 1937.

Tabletop Sparton radio fashioned from cobalt-blue mirror and ebonized wood with chrome-metal strips. Designed by Walter Dorwin Teague in the automotive-Moderne style for Sparks-Withington Co., Jackson, Michigan, 1936.

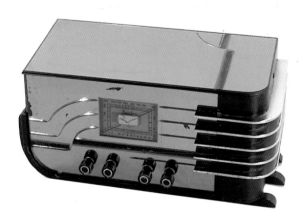

Table-model yellow Marblette radio in lyre shape, manufactured by DeWald, ca. 1938.

Baby tabletop General Electric radio in brown marbleized Bakelite, ca. 1934.

Moderne-style RCA Victor table-model console radio designed by John Vassos, in wood veneer with steel chrome cradle.

Blue-mirrored Sparton "Bluebird" table-model radio on a black-lacquered wooden base with chromium auto-style decoration and three chromium-strip streamlines. Designed by Walter Dorwin Teague and made by Sparks-Withington Co., 1936. This radio is prominently featured in Born to Dance (1936) in the penthouse scene in which Virginia Bruce sings "I've Got You Under My Skin" to a bashful Jimmy Stewart.

Radio for the Millions *book with dust jacket published by Grosset & Dunlap and printed by arrangement with the Popular Science Publishing Co., Inc., copyright 1945.*

RCA Victor console radio in black-lacquer cabinet supported by chromium-plated tubular-steel framework, designed by industrial designer John Vassos, ca. 1935.

mirror with chromium strips and black-enameled wood for some of these luxurious streamlined showpieces that usually were seen only in penthouses, in the homes of Hollywood movie stars, and in the lounges of luxury hotels.

RCA Victor hired industrial designer John Vassos to design moderne-style radios and phonographs. Highly prized by today's collectors, these radios captivated the American public during the Depression and World War II. For many middle-class families, there had to be one in the living room and another in the kitchen—as well as in the bedrooms and the den.

THE PLASTIC INEVITABLE

New "art" plastics came into popular usage through the efforts of industrial designers in the 1930s and are the chief reason so many Deco collectors today seek out Catalin radios at antique markets and in hundreds of stores from coast to coast that sell the "new antiques" of the twentieth century. In fact, many major galleries and museums have come to regard items made of this early plastic as one of the key aspects of design in the 1920s and '30s.

Alexander Parkes, an Englishman, produced the first commercial plastic, a cellulose nitrate, in 1855. Calling his chemical discovery Parkesine, he exhibited this new material in the form of buttons, pens, combs, and other objects at the 1862 International Exhibition, where he was given an achievement medal. This plastic was viewed as a low-cost substitute for natural materials like tortoiseshell, ivory, and amber, but its full potential was not realized until the turn of the century.

A synthetic plastic called Pyroxylin was invented in 1868 by John Wesley Hyatt as a possible material to be used in cheaply manufacturing billiard balls, which were then made of ivory. The Pyroxylin formula, which came to be known as Celluloid, was flammable, thin, soft, and brittle and proved woefully inadequate for billiards. Later, the "celluloid" brand of plastic was produced by the Celluloid Corporation of New York for use in thousands of products. Celluloid was utilized in nitrate film stock, and the term "cel," which characterizes cartoon images hand-painted on celluloid for animated films, was derived from this brand name. Another lightweight plastic was manufactured under the brand name Nixonoid at the Nixon Nitration Works in Nixon, New Jersey; Nacara was made by Fiberloid Corporation of Indian Orchard, Massachusetts.

Phenol formaldehyde is the basic compound for 1930s plastics highly regarded and collected as "art" plastic today. Brand names for this early type of phenolic resin are Bakelite, Catalin, Durez, Durite, Agatine, Gemstone, and Marblette.

Bar- and game-room accessories in the Depression might have included this novelty Catalin dice box with plastic chips and a red Catalin dice table lighter.

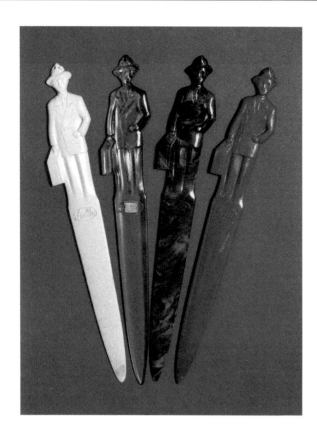

added "inner light," these radios actually appeared luminescent in a dimly lit room.

Celluloid, Catalin, Bakelite, Pyralin, Fiberloid, Nixonoid, Tenite, Plastacele, Ameroid, Vinylite, Coltrock, Durez, Durite, Insurok, Indur, Makalot, Resinox, Textolite, Arcolite, Marblette, Ivaleur, Micarta, Formica, Lamicoid, Panelyte, Synthane, Dilecto, Phenolite, and Spauldite were some of the "plastics" of the 1930s—the list went on. The five *main* groups, however, were the following:

1. Pyroxylin—the celluloids.
2. Phenolics—Bakelite and Catalin.
3. Urea formaldehyde—a cheaper composition plastic with product brand names that included Plaskon, Uralite, Duroware, Hemcoware, and one particular brand, Beatl, that in its Beetleware line manufactured the immensely popular Little Orphan Annie Ovaltine shake-up mugs and other radio premiums.
4. Casein—used mainly for buttons and buckles, furniture knobs, and shade pulls.
5. Cellulose acetate—as Tenite and Similoid, it had flexibility and translucence and was used primarily for steering wheels, on dashboards, and for automobile knobs and window and door handles. It could be molded but not cast; and due to its brittleness and hardness, it often cracked with use.

It is Catalin, however, with its smooth finish, high luster, and durability, that was the most desirable brand of plastic for radios and costume jewelry. Its many translucent and opaque colors made it preferable to Bakelite for decoratives, although by 1938 the Bakelite manufacturers were able to introduce some colors and added ivory and white to their line of plastics. A 1936 *Fortune* magazine article referred, in jest, to Catalin as "the gaudy brother of Bakelite."

There were literally hundreds of early plastic brand names used in mass production, and these, in combi-

Leo Hendrick Baekeland discovered the basic formula for a sturdy plastic that could be cast and molded by machinery in 1909. Named after the inventor and later produced by Union Carbide, Bakelite is usually a dark brown or maroon and was used in many of the early Art Deco table-model radios as well as in other items of good industrial design. The American Catalin Corporation of New York called its new plastic, Catalin, "The Gem of Modern Industry," for it could be molded with practicability into many shapes and could be produced in a wide range of colors. Bright butterscotch yellows, scarlet reds, orange, violet blue, marbleized greens, maroon, white, and amber were frequently used colors for radio cabinetry and as decorative accents. Sometimes, with the combination of the dial bulb, the glow from the tubes, and an

INSUROK

the superior plastic by Richardson is available in sheets, rods, tubes, punchings and other forms, both molded and laminated, for fabrication in your plant, or in completely finished parts ready for assembly. Richardson facilities encompass the use of Bakelite Beetle, Durez, Plaskon, Resinox, Tenite and other forms of synthetic resin plastics. Literature and INSUROK catalogues on request.

Radio by Belmont Radio Corp., Chicago, Ill.

The RICHARDSON COMPANY

Melrose Park, (Chicago) Ill.   *Founded 1858*   Lockland, (Cincinnati) Ohio
New Brunswick, N. J.   Indianapolis, Ind.
Detroit: 6-252 G. M. Building. Phone, Madison 9386   New York: 75 West Street. Phone, Whitehall 4-4687

Insurok, a synthetic resin plastic, used for a radio made by Belmont Radio Corporation of Chicago, Illinois.

nation with other elements, such as chromium and aluminum, provided inspiration for Loewy, Weber, Deskey, Vassos, Rohde, Bel Geddes, Harold Van Doren, George Fred Keck, and the others who designed with the machine and volume-marketing always in mind. Practical and decorative parts for toasters, lamps, and cocktail accessories were often fashioned in Catalin or Bakelite. Streamlining based on airstream concepts (i.e., aerodynamics) needed the new materials as well as new designs to attract customers in the Depression era.

The Bakelite Pavilion at the New York World's Fair of 1939 showed myriad uses for plastics in the world of consumerism, and each visitor was presented with a tiny orange-and-blue Trylon and Perisphere pin embossed "BAKELITE."

Stupendous jukeboxes also used a rainbow assortment of Catalin and Bakelite along with wood or Lucite, which is a sturdy, clear acrylic used in furnishings and other decorative items. The primary reason for collecting early plastic table radios or jukeboxes has to do not only with their styling but the obsolete lustrous plastics used in their manufacture. Wooden radios of high-Deco styling are also sought-after pieces in this new design-conscious arena, but the bright Popsicle colors and sleek contours of early plastic radios have thrust them into the limelight. Fada, Emerson, Arvin, Bendix, Crosley, DeWald, Philco, Garod, RCA Victor, Cyart, Air King, Stewart-Warner, and Majestic are but a few of the beautiful "Baby" radios designed in the 1930s to brighten up the bedroom vanity or the kitchen countertop. Startlingly, these "Pee Wees" were referred to in a 1933 *Fortune* article as accounting for 300,000 sales out of a total of 500,000 radios sold between December 1, 1932, and May 1, 1933.

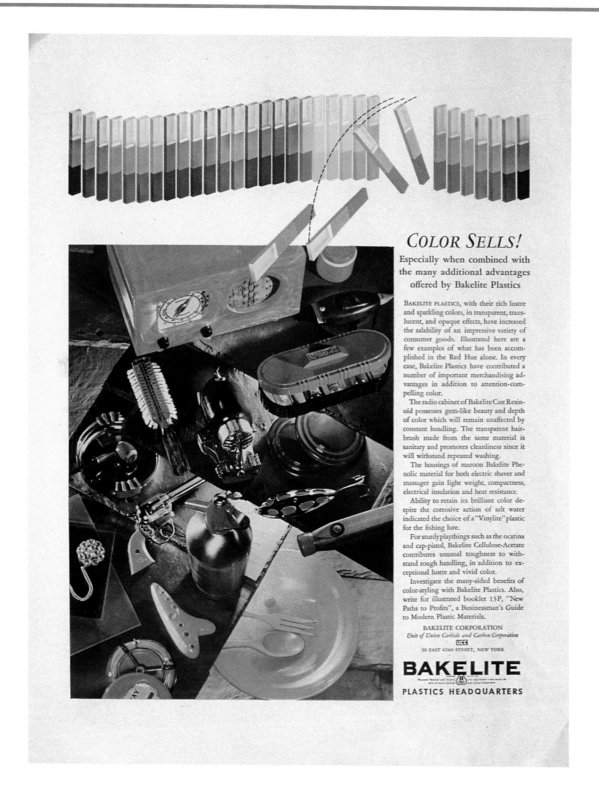

Assortment of Bakelite objects from the Bakelite Corporation of New York. Fortune, February 1940.

Red Catalin belt buckle on original card.

Dime Store Deco Jewels

From the last decades of the nineteenth century on into the early 1920s, 40,000 tons of celluloid were produced each year for the manufacture of combs, letter openers, bracelets, barrettes, hair ornaments, pendants, imitation cameos, belt and shoe buckles, vanity sets, and dress, hat, and stick pins. Popular-priced novelty costume jewelry was also made of Bakelite, Galalith, or Aladdinite. As cheaply produced imitations of tortoiseshell, ivory, bone, and amber, these early plastics satisfied a large public and flooded the marketplace.

At the 1925 Paris exposition most of the exquisite necklaces, bracelets, and brooches exhibited by reigning European jewelry designers were fashioned of the traditional platinum, gold, silver, diamonds, sapphires, emeralds, rubies, and other gemstones. In contrast, Deco-design celluloid jewelry of this period was often inlaid with rhinestone and marcasite for a glittering effect that manufacturers associated with the new jazzy styles of the twenties.

When the Crash of 1929 was felt in world jewelry markets, the value of expensive precious stones and metals also plummeted, and many of the previously well-to-do were forced to sell their treasures back to dealers for much less than they paid for them. At this low economic point, novelty plastic jewelry moved into a wide-open market with great success. It was

Clip-on "Genuine Catalin" orange dress buckle on original card.

also at this time that Catalin, as the preferred substance, began to supersede Celluloid. The more durable Catalin was buffed and highly polished in the factory process and came in an array of sun-bright colors that seemed to ward off the stock market doldrums. Ladies who had had to pawn their luxury bangles and baubles now, just for the fun of it, wandered into Saks or Bonwits to pick up inexpensive pieces of Catalin plastic jewelry. So popular was this mass-produced Catalin that it accounted for 50 percent of jewelry sales in the 1930s.

For jewelry, the Deco style was extremely marketable. Some intricate jewelry designs were especially created with Catalin in mind, not to combine it with fake stones, as in the twenties, but with glamorous industrial metals like chrome, aluminum, brass, and even glazed ceramics and wood. Some high-style Deco motifs were fashioned by imaginative designers

into pieces for women now looking for something striking and vibrant to wear on a coat, dress, or suit-jacket lapel. Color in two or more coordinated combinations, like yellow with red and ebony, could be used to create exciting Deco effects.

Catalin "chunk" bracelets were produced in the hundreds of thousands each year, with some of them also carved on lathes in attractive patterns. Separate plastic runs of single or mixed colors were strung together as accordion bracelets and combined in an artful manner with chromium balls or clear Lucite triangular shapes.

Novelty Catalin dress clips or sweater pins in the 1930s could have a whimsical side. Clusters of red cherries with green leaves on a big red chunk of plastic radiated a show-business glitz that was anything but subtle. *Modern Plastics* of February 1939 featured "novelty dress adornments" in a variety of shapes, sizes, and colors from stock molds, including the popular Scottie dog and horse's head as subjects. Other shapes for Catalin jewelry included fish, birds, does, leaping gazelles, cowboy boots, hats and guns, insects, Cubist-style African heads, and hearts, as well as carved leaf, floral, and geometric patterns. The variety was endless. If these pieces were combined with metal chains, studs, or chromium strips, if they were hand-painted, or if glass eyes were added to an animal's head, the production expense would be passed on to the consumer.

Handsome three-horse hookup belt buckle in carved Catalin.

Carved Catalin horsehead dress pin with glass eye insert.

Dress pin in green and black Catalin with chromium studs and rings.

Catalin clips, pins, rings, and belt buckles also turned up at the dime store in the 1930s, hence the term "dime store Deco" or "Junque Jewelry," which is sometimes used in conjunction with vintage plastic jewelry. Often a pair of matching clips on a cardboard was sold for 10¢ at the five-and-dime store with the imprint "CATALIN JEWELRY" right on the card.

Cast phenolic resin plastic (i.e., Catalin and Bakelite) was employed in the making of a variety of novelty objects, including napkin rings in the shape of birds, Scotties, rabbits, or elephants, or the World's Fair Trylon and Perisphere symbol, salt and pepper sets, table lighters, cigarette holders, cigarette boxes, midget pencil sharpeners (often with a decal appliqué of Mickey Mouse, Popeye, or Dick Tracy affixed), clocks, vanity boxes, face powder containers, and thermometer stands. Practical plastic items included shaving brushes, toothbrushes, hand razors, letter openers, fountain pens, desk sets, tool handles, kitchen flatware, and drink tumblers. A voluminous array of buttons, a good number of them interesting and collectible, were made in the shape of fruit, vegetables, birds, animals, sailboats, anchors, or even Snow White and all of the Seven Dwarfs.

The plastic inevitable, as Andy Warhol referred to it in the 1960s, had first roared in with a vengeance in the 1930s, making itself known on everything from handbag clasps and shoe and belt buckles to door handles, poker chips, and dice. The plastic revolution has not been countered to this day. A world without plastic is now unthinkable, which is why these early plastic forms and the beginnings of mass plastic production are so important to us. In the early eighties the production of plastics worldwide overtook that of steel; what once was seen as "inevitable" is now here to stay: the Age of Plastic!

Chunky carved Catalin bracelets.

Deco clear Lucite animal and bird dress pins were popular items in the 1930s, '40s, and '50s.

PUTTIN' ON THE RITZ

When we envision a 1920s and '30s Deco life-style, the images that most readily come to mind are not usually associated with the middle-class homebody sensibility, or the breadlines of the Depression, or hungry men chanting "Brother, Can You Spare a Dime?" while they try to sell apples on a street corner. To be sure, this was a time of social crisis and despair, but what entices us most today in terms of Art Deco would be scenes of beautiful, svelte ladies in form-fitting white, red, or black satin gowns and draped in fox furs, on the arms of handsome gentlemen in top hat, tux, and sporting walking sticks, arriving in long, sleek chauffeur-driven Packard limousines at the theater or a "Hottentot" Broadway or Hollywood nightclub.

The writer Helen Lawrenson, in an essay for *Esquire* magazine, described an incident in which she and *Vogue* publisher Condé Nast, in high evening attire, were in just such a car on their way to a Park Avenue cocktail party when the ride was suddenly interrupted by angry men demanding attention who pounded on the car and rocked it back and forth. Shouting obscenities at the smartly dressed twosome, these on-strike workers finally allowed the chauffeur, with his aristocratic passengers aghast and badly shaken, to proceed. It was the first real encounter for these haughty literary intellectuals with the trials and tribulations of the out-of-work. Stylish magazines chose to ignore the effects of the Great Depression in America, and *Vanity Fair* once even took to describing Adolf Hitler as a mere annoyance, a sheep in wolf's clothing.

Gotham high-hat glamour is mockingly portrayed in the Busby Berkeley "Lullabye of Broadway" sequence in the movie musical *Gold Diggers of 1935*, where dozens of tap dancers chase a Broadway baby—Winifred Shaw—up a flight of nightclub stairs and accidentally cause her to fall out of an unlocked glass door to her death on a Broadway street many dizzying stories below. Alice Faye sang "Slumming on Park Avenue" in *On the Avenue* in 1937 and often appeared

Twenty-four girls in see-through hoop dresses and Ruby Keeler in a platinum wig all played electrified white neon violins in the black-and-white musical Gold Diggers of 1933 *directed by Busby Berkeley. Rare Warner Bros. prop violin used in "Shadow Waltz" sequence is from the collection of Kenneth Anger.*

STYLED BY HOWARD

in "radio" films like *Wake Up and Live* and *The Great American Broadcast*, which featured Art Deco radio-studio and nightclub settings. These opulent Deco-style movies, and many other musicals and screwball comedies like them, portrayed life on the fringes of well-to-do society where the nobs took show girls and boys along for a ride while "painting the town red."

Nightclubs in New York like the El Morocco with its zebra-skin decor, the Stork Club, Billy Rose's Diamond Horseshoe, the Kit Kat Club, and Sardi's; Chicago's Aragon Ballroom and Congress Casino; or the Trocadero, the "It" Club, the Coconut Grove, the Brown Derby,

and the Mocambo in Hollywood attracted the famous, beauteous, and adventuresome with the magic of their glamorous moderne surroundings.

Hotel dance orchestras like Guy Lombardo and his Royal Canadians at the Roosevelt Grill, Leo Reisman's at the Central Park Casino, Enric Madriguera and his Hotel Biltmore Orchestra, Paul Whiteman at the Biltmore Roof Garden, Emil Petti and his Savoy-Plaza Orchestra, Anson Weeks and his Hotel Mark Hopkins Orchestra, George Hall and his Taft Hotel Orchestra featuring Dolly Dawn and her Dawn Patrol, Gus Arnheim and his Coconut Grove Ambassador Hotel Orchestra, Rich-

Original Stork Club matchbook cover. Sherman Billingsley's famous nightclub and gathering spot for celebrities was at 3 East 53rd Street in New York City.

WORDS WITHOUT MUSIC

Rainbow Room matchbook cover, 1930s, Rockefeller Center, New York.

Sheet music from Ziegfeld Follies of 1936.

The ultramodern Lounge Cafe in the Waldorf-Astoria in 1935, with chromium furnishings and mirrored bar.

ties, hats, and polished shoes, and ladies were always well attired in a hat with veil, gloves, a smart dress, coat, and stylish heels. Good form in appearance and an upbeat attitude were essential ingredients for survival in the Deco-Depression age.

In 1931 the Broadway musical *Face the Music* introduced Irving Berlin's song, "Let's Have Another Cup of Coffee, Let's Have Another Piece of Pie." Performed on a set designed to duplicate a New York Automat, the lyrics optimistically avowed that trouble was just a bubble and the clouds would soon roll by. If you whistled, hummed, or sang the musical messages of the 1930s, "Keep Your Sunny Side Up," "Painting the Clouds with Sunshine," "Singin' in the Rain," "If I Had a Million Dollars," "Life Is Just a Bowl of Cherries," "You're the Cream in My Coffee," "On a Choo-Choo Heading for Better Times," "With Plenty of Money and You," "We're in the Money," "Pennies from Heaven," "There's a New Day Coming," "Where the Blue of the Night Meets the Gold of the Day," "I Found a Million Dollar Baby at the Five and Ten Cent Store," "Wake Up and Live," and "Make Way for Kid

ard Himber and his Ritz-Carlton Hotel Orchestra, and other groups like those of Jimmie Grier, Isham Jones, Eddie Duchin, and Ozzie Nelson epitomize the "Deco sound" in music.

Hot nights in Harlem were considered daring and outré in the 1920s and '30s. Dancing at the Cotton Club on Lenox Avenue and 142nd Street to the zippy jazz sounds of Duke Ellington's or Cab "Hi-de-ho" Calloway's bands often led to all-night party affairs. If it were not the Plantation Club or Connie's Inn, it was the Savoy Ballroom where Fats Waller played boogie-woogie on the ivories and Billie Holiday or Ella Fitzgerald sang songs that were sometimes red-hot and sometimes blue.

The 1930s was an elegant time, by night or by day. For daytime wear, city men invariably donned suits,

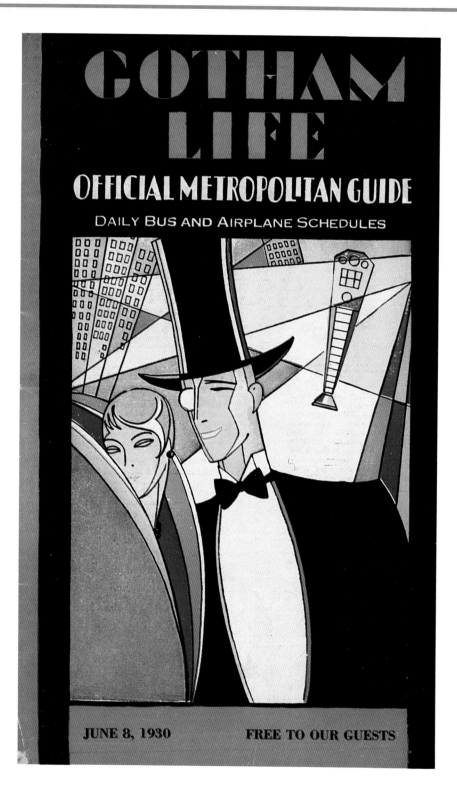

Gotham Life, *guide to New York for week of June 8, 1930. Broadway shows one could see included* Simple Simon *with "10¢-a-dance-singer"* Ruth Etting, Strike Up the Band, *and* Hotel Universe.

After "Repeal" smart cocktail lounges opened everywhere in cities across America. These Deco matchbook graphics depict elegant gentlemen and their ladies engaged in sophisticated fun on the town.

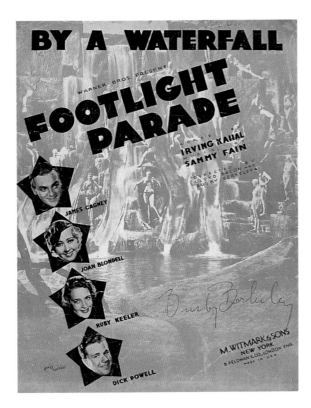

Prosperity," you could theoretically keep that Big Bad Wolf from the door.

If you could not afford the luxury of "Puttin' on the Ritz," which the majority of Americans could not in the 1930s, you might content yourself by listening to "Grand Central Station," "The Mysterious Traveler," or "Mr. First-Niter" with Les Tremayne on the radio, or by playing 78 rpm records of your favorite crooners on the Victrola. Staying at home reading a novel or looking at magazine pictures and ads showing high-hat gentlemen and their sophisticated ladies on the town helped provide momentary escape. If there was not a real rainbow with a pot of money "just over the hill" or "just around the bend," as promised in songs of the day, then perhaps by the end of the Depression in 1939 happiness might be found in a futuristic emerald green Art Deco all-in-technicolor Fantasy City just down the yellow brick road—in a place called Oz. Hollywood movies offered up the ultimate vicarious experience and escape in pictures like *The Wizard of Oz* or *Gone With the Wind*. And then there were the world's fairs of 1939 in San Francisco and New York that promised a better tomorrow and gave middle-class families hope for the dawning of a new day.

Sheet music for "I've Got to Sing a Torch Song" from the Warner Bros. musical film Gold Diggers of 1933, *featuring Ginger Rogers on the cover.*

"By a Waterfall," words by Irving Cahal, music by Sammy Fain, personally autographed by Busby Berkeley.

Cosmetics Packaging

The development of mass media advertising in the 1920s, the impact of the 1925 Paris exposition upon the world of graphic design, and the increase in product endorsement by glamorous and influential Hollywood stars in the 1930s combined to make Art Deco the primary style in modern, sophisticated packaging design for cosmetics products. Women in the 1920s and '30s were seeking a modern image; so, for the powder box, the talcum tin, the cold cream jar, or the perfume bottle, modernism became an essential element in spurring new sales. Prior to the twenties, cosmetics were mainly used by stage actors, vaudeville performers, or wanton women; what once was regarded as ''a painted face'' now was genteelly referred to as ''makeup for madame.'' Max Factor of Hollywood, who created ''The New Art of Society Makeup,'' said in 1928, ''The expression 'paint and powder' and the criticism of a 'painted' appearance may be attributed to a wrong understanding and the incorrect use of makeup.''

''Makeup'' was a relatively new term, coined by the cosmetics industry, and women took readily to the notion of learning how to utilize beauty hints from experts like Mr. Factor or Westmore of Hollywood. Representatives of these cosmetics firms appeared at the dime store or the department store hawking products by demonstrating for women shoppers the

The ''Deco Look''—lips, lashes, hair, eyebrows, and fingernails—on Warner Bros. Hollywood starlet Carole Hughes.

correct way to apply makeup for just the right effect. The effect was not necessarily toward a more natural look; instead, it emulated the Hollywood images of stars like Garbo, Lombard, Dietrich, or Crawford. This meant, by 1930s standards: high-arched pencil-thin brows drawn sometimes almost as a semicircle; black-mascaraed eyelashes; blue, green, or violet eye shadow; bright red lips, often painted over the lip line for a fuller effect; dry or cream rouge applied to cheeks over a pancake base and followed by tinted powder—all together combining in an almost masklike mythic and artificial appearance. To the many women who chose to adopt the "modern face" created by cosmetics, makeup was an entrée into a fantasy world of glamour and allure they previously had only dreamt of. Men were attracted to the new provocative woman now encountered everywhere, smoking ciga- rettes and wearing red lipstick not just on the street but in the office, at the cocktail bar, and in social encounters at the country club.

Hairstyles for women went from the short Clara Bow–Louise Brooks 1920s bob to a more streamlined

Princess Pat duotone rouge case (which sold for 10¢) in "Tango" orange, a fashionable color of the 1920s and '30s. Princess Pat Ltd., Chicago, Illinois.

Screenland magazine, February 1924, features beautiful stage and silent-screen actress Marion Davies in portrait by famed illustrator Rolf Armstrong.

Opposite: Beauty parlor booklet that opens up to show the variety of Clairol hair-color samples, from jet black to flame red to sable brown to silver blonde, copyright Clairol, Inc., Stamford, Connecticut, 1939.

The Moderne Method, the story of beauty culture and its development, published by A. B Moler, Chicago, 1931.

Tangee dry-rouge container, lithographed face-powder tins, and cardboard containers, shown with lipstick tube in black-and-red Bakelite with its original box. All five-and-dime cosmetics from George W. Luft Co., Fifth Avenue, New York, 1930s and '40s.

close-to-the-head coiffure with machine-set waves or dips. The sculptured "Marcel" permanent wave, named after the French hairdresser Marcel Grateau, its originator, drove every Depression shop girl, housewife, and precious little girl straight to their local beauty shoppe for an "electric permanent." The early contraptions used in this process were complicated, and operators had to be very attentive to timing lest they singe the hair or worse. Rollers were electrified from one central unit, which often looked like the operating table and machinery used to zap, awaken, and curl Elsa Lanchester's hair in *The Bride of Frankenstein*. Mother left the beauty parlor in a hairnet to preserve her tight waves and crimp curls styled after Ginger Rogers or Kay Francis, while the little girl came out in corkscrew curls looking like Shirley Temple.

Platinumizing with a white henna peroxide compound to match movie-star Jean Harlow's hair color became a fad in the thirties; products like Blondex Shampoo, Marchand's Golden Hair Wash, Golden Glint Rinse Shampoo, and Lady Clairol products offered women the opportunity for a "lighter, brighter life" through blonder hair. Toby Wing, Lyda Roberti, Betty Grable, Alice Faye, and all of Busby Berkeley's *Gold Digger* chorines went "platinum," a term suggested by the precious white metal and coined by Howard Hughes for his protégé Harlow. There is little doubt that the Deco look for ladies, be they blonde, brunette, or redhead, was created and mythologized by Hollywood, and women were going for it all the way at the makeup counter or the corner drugstore.

"The Beauty Business has swept the country in the last decade with a speed no less astounding than the radio, refrigerator or road-building industries." So declared *Fortune* magazine in August 1930. The world of cosmetics in that year had become a two billion dollar business, with advertising budgets going appre-

ciably higher than those for food products or automobiles. Advertising graphics had to appeal to the moderne trend in every conceivable area of the marketplace. Representations of female features and body countours in fashion ads also had to be highly stylized and streamlined, in keeping with this trend.

The product look in powder compacts and rouge pots for companies like Djer Kiss, Trejur, Tangee, Princess Pat, Outdoor Girl, or Max Factor was attractively presented in the Art Deco style of geometric patterns embellished with floral images or sunburst motifs.

Movie and beauty magazines and special cosmetic booklets contained inspiring beauty messages, tips, and "Secrets from the Stars to You," and fashion periodicals that once stressed only women's apparel now included "how to" articles on the correct application of beauty products. Advertisements appealed to the desire to become beautiful, and some were not above exaggerated claims for their particular cosmetic brand. Products like "Jungle Savage" lipstick and nail polish; Norma's "Kissable" lipstick—"Hollywood's Latest Sensation"—in raspberry and "vivid" poppy;

Small enamel-and-chrome rouge-powder compact for the purse in striking Deco design.

Winx eye beautifiers; Maybelline mascara, eyeshadow, and eyebrow pencils; Richard Hudnut powder and rouge; and Lady Esther cold creams often used suggestive, alluring ads that subliminally promised women adventures like a tropical romance on a South Sea island. Fantasy and fact did not always coincide, but this did not matter in a burgeoning market that was bent on selling perfection.

The Queen of the cosmetics industry in the thirties was Elizabeth Arden, who along with promoting her Ardena Velva Creme, astringents, Venetian Orange Skin Food, and an extensive line of makeup also opened a Fifth Avenue beauty salon similar to the one caricatured in Claire Booth Luce's *The Women*. The jaunty M-G-M film version of the successful Broadway comedy starred Norma Shearer, Joan Crawford, Rosalind Russell, Paulette Goddard, and Joan Fontaine as the bitchy group who were "made over" in an elaborate beauty palace with exercise rooms, muscle strapping devices, steam, massage, skin toning, and full hair, manicure, and makeup treatments. Elizabeth Arden specialized in advice on how to counteract skin

Small powder compact made of celluloid and chromium. Karess product for F. W. Woolworth & Co., New York, 1929.

Deco packaging: Radio Girl face-powder box manufactured by the Belco Co., St. Paul, Minnesota, ca. 1934.

dryness, dirtiness, wrinkles, crow's-feet and in pre-
serving or restoring that "youthful" complexion.

Madame Helena Rubinstein, one of seven Russian
sisters from Cracow, was Arden's direct competitor,
and she claimed to have originated the idea of the
beauty salon. She opened Rubinstein shops in several
countries that sold her own specialty products, such
as Chinese Red Lipstick and Rouge, powders, lash
enhancers, and Persian Mascara.

Coty, Colgate-Palmolive-Peet, Procter and Gamble,
Lever Brothers, and Pond's all cashed in by competing
in the "complexion soap" market. No longer did
Procter and Gamble produce only their 99 and 44/100th
percent pure "floating" Ivory Soap. In the 1930s they
introduced Camay "complexion" soap for "delicate
skin." By then many women had perceived that Ivory
Soap, which celebrated its 100th year in 1937, was too
fatty and harsh; they demanded a soap product with
olive oil, oatmeal, or some other smoothing agent
added. Complexion soap packaging and advertising
also had to go modern in the 1930s.

Fragrance was to become an important element in
soaps and creams. Cosmetics firms like the American
Coty (an adjunct of the French firm), Houbigant, D'Orsay,
Guerlain, Yardley, DeVilbiss, and others had long been
leaders in the scent market, selling perfume and eau
de cologne in beautiful Deco-styled bottles with fanciful French names, but it took American mass-production
advertising and distribution techniques to fully exploit
the sweet smell of lavender or the tincture of roses as
essential to all women everywhere.

Deco packaging, created to appeal to a modern
world that was going full speed ahead in the 1930s,
was not limited to cosmetics and toiletries alone.
Although the cosmetics industry led the way, attractive package design in this modern style may be found
on cookie and cracker tins, hardware nail tins, type-

Skyscraper-style glass perfume bottle, Narcisse de Paris Parfum, 1928.

Roja Brilliantine Hair Lotion for streamlining sleek, mod-ern plastered-down hairstyles for men and women, manu-factured in Paris.

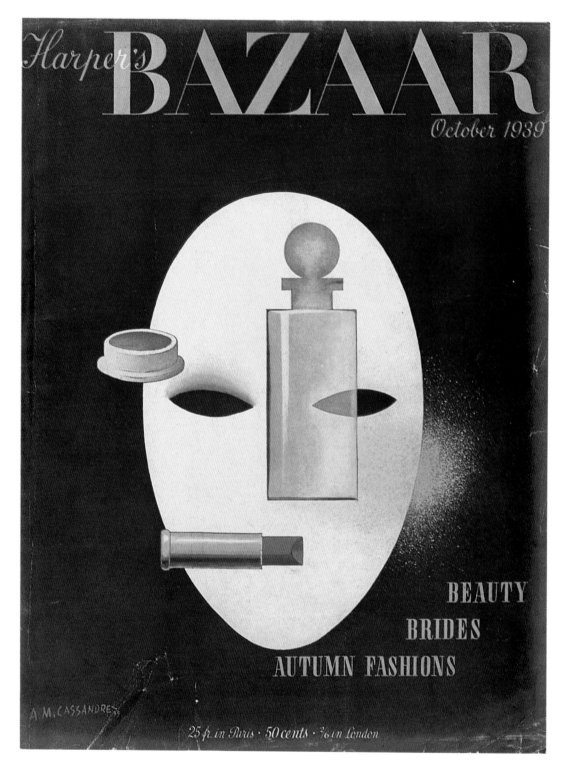

Sweet Gardenia perfumed talcum-powder tin in floral Art Deco pattern. Lander Perfumer, Binghamton, Memphis, New York.

writer ribbon and phonograph needle tins, incense boxes, needle and sewing packages, spice, coffee, and tea packages, toothpaste tubes and cartons, cigarette and pipe mixture packs, and hair tonic containers, laundry detergent boxes, soda pop bottles, and countless other products that went "modernistic" in the twenties, thirties, and later as either brand-new products or as old ones redesigned. Some, of course, did not readily change due to a strong product-identification imprint on the public—such old stand-bys as Cream of Wheat, Quaker Oats, Aunt Jemima Pancake Mix, Ovaltine, Log Cabin Syrup, Campbell's Soup, Old Dutch Cleanser, and Bon Ami Powder.

Wrigley's Chewing Gum, which was a forerunner in unique modern packaging and smartly air-brushed

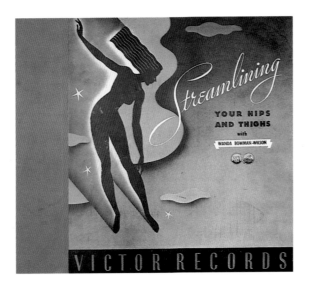

"Streamlining Your Hips and Thighs" by Wanda Bowman-Wilson, an RCA Victor 78rpm record album outlining course of exercise for the modern woman who wanted to emulate svelte Hollywood stars like Greta Garbo, Katharine Hepburn, and Carole Lombard.

advertisements, also attempted to make a pitch to beauty-conscious women, stating what the company called "An Old Beauty Secret": "Keep lips young, and you keep them pretty. And, one of the oldest and most inexpensive Beauty Secrets for this is merely chewing gum from the Sapota tree, the beauty tree of ancient Mexico, which is what you have in Wrigley's. Chew Wrigley's at least ten minutes a day. Note the added loveliness in texture and contour that gradually finds its alluring way to your lips."

Princess Pat lipstick tube on original card was sold at dime store cosmetic counters in the 1930s. Princess Pat, Ltd., Chicago, Illinois.

Deco Graphics

Paper ephemera, yesterday's magazines, newspapers, souvenir menus, and matchbooks from an exact point in time—day, month, year—can evoke the mood of a particular period, a long-ago event, or release more ecstatic feelings in those who really were there and still "remember." An old picture postcard becomes a memory-treasure for the many people who collect them. Usually stamped and dated on the message side, they often have a friendly handwritten "hello" or "wish you were here" from mothers, fathers, aunts, uncles, cousins, friends, or sweethearts who now may have disappeared off the face of the earth. Early magazines, each in its own special area—Hollywood, world news, fashion, sports, or home furnishings—can likewise arouse powerful nostalgic yearnings for the past, even in someone who never actually lived through those times. Specific symbols and images of days-gone-by can startle, even thrust the reader into another era, in which, for a moment, he remains captivated. This is certainly true not only when we listen to an old-time recording by Bessie Smith or Vaughn de Leath but when we see advertisements from bygone times, pick up the sheet music of a favorite song, or read an article about the Depression in a 1933 *Time* or *Fortune* magazine.

An ordinary cardboard matchbook advertising the Cotton Club, the Coconut Grove, the Chicago World's

Fair of 1933, a highway tourist-cabin motor court, or a diner-eatery and gas station road stop not only represents the era from which it came; it is a miniature piece of popular graphic art that often employed fine design and printing. Many of these are executed in a Deco-design style of the 1920s and '30s when an ad on a matchbook for a nightclub, a can of soup, or a brand of cigarettes was still a novel and extremely potent way of getting the message across.

Popular prints, magazine advertisements, company brochures and booklets, radio premium send-aways and photos, playing cards, trading cards, baseball cards, movie-star cigarette-insert cards, greeting cards, bridge scorecards, postage stamps, fruit and vegetable box labels, cigar labels, political pamphlets, and travel, product, and movie posters, lobby cards, movie

scene stills, advertising ink blotters, and road maps are often excellent resources for examining the techniques of modern graphics and illustrations from the "Golden Age" of printing.

Many of the specific paper categories have well-established collector organizations and study groups who gather together to establish the rarity of individual pieces. Postage stamps, comic books, baseball cards, travel posters, and movie memorabilia are lead subjects, all of which have periodic meetings and conventions, publish newsletters, and have networks of hard-core collectors who help establish values for the things collected. These topics are also popular subjects for books and price guides. In this sense, graphics in any number of paper categories have become an important aspect of viewing the world of Art Deco in the print media.

Dust jackets on popular novels and illustrated books of the period form a chief category in which to find good examples of Deco design. American book illustrators such as Rockwell Kent, Lynd Ward, and John Vassos worked in block prints or black-and-white lithography; these men also created ads for various products like paint, perfume, or automobiles. Rockwell Kent also designed his own book plates, Christmas cards, and book covers, and created a variety of prints for framing. Lynd Ward illustrated over 100 adult and juvenile books in a variety of media: pen-and-ink, brush drawing, watercolor, wash, oil, lithography, woodcuts, and mezzotints. He became famous for his visualist novels *God's Man*, *Mad Man's Drum*, and *Vertigo*, which were told entirely without words in modernistic black-and-white woodcuts. John Vassos, with his wife Ruth, created books with dynamic exaggerated avant-garde Deco illustrations. *Contempo*, *Ultimo*, *Humanities*, and *Phobia* are highly desirable compendiums of the Art Deco style as it applies to

Deco-graphic playing card, from King Press, Inc., Carlstadt, New Jersey.

Box of fifty bookplates with Lynd Ward design "Harvest," Antioch Bookplate Co., Yellow Springs, Ohio.

Opposite: Wings, *literary periodical, July 1929, featuring on the cover Rockwell Kent's* Flame.

illustrated books. Vassos, who was also a stage, modern-interior, and industrial designer, heightened editions of Oscar Wilde's *Salomé, The Ballad of Reading Gaol*, and *The Harlot's House*, and Gray's *Elegy* and Coleridge's *Kubla Kahn* with his startling symbolic illustration techniques.

Excellent Deco graphics and drawings can sometimes be found in period high school and university yearbooks from the twenties and thirties. Regional books, tourist information booklets, bus, plane, and train timetables, and travel-guide brochures are fascinating records of evolving transportation methods. Automotive, motor, and aeronautics booklets, as well as hobby and mechanics magazines, often had Deco

fantasy illustrations on their covers, conveying a futuristic vision with jutting skyscrapers, factories, highways, and bridges that reach across meadows and rivers toward the open horizon. Some depicted streamlined futuristic Dymaxion cars or other imaginative science-fiction jet-stream vehicles speeding down the highway or whirling through space like comets or flying saucers.

New color lithography processes, inks, and paper production methods improved the technical quality of books published, as well as magazines and other graphics. In magazine production no publication was more eloquent than *Fortune*, which demanded that advertisers create ads of high-quality design that appealed to the idea of merging artistic merit with industry's needs in a modern age. In its first few years (*Fortune* premiered in February 1930) the magazine reported on the fads and foibles of the wealthy and privileged classes; its $1 cover price throughout the decade certainly restricted it to the more influential and affluent reader. In 1935 the magazine that boasted more advertising than any other monthly in the world began its quarterly "Poll of the Common Man," which significantly helped to shift the editorial focus toward more progressive humanitarian concerns. By 1938 this poll and its attendant surveys appeared monthly and was widely regarded as an accurate barometer of public opinion. To look at a 1930s *Fortune* from today's viewpoint is to see a total achievement of quality design and execution that is seldom equaled in the current world of magazine graphics.

Another prominent illustrator who contributed to the formulation of Deco style was Maxfield Parrish, whose "Air Castles" cover for *Ladies Home Journal* appeared in 1903. His medieval fantasy illustrations, featuring clowns, nude nymphets, knaves and jesters, biblical and fairy-tale characters, castles in the clouds, bubble kingdoms, mythical mountain ranges, spectacular sunsets, mysterious lakes and dark forests, many bathed in his famous "Maxfield Parrish Blue," were seen in dozens of American publications. The famous Parrish framed prints were ubiquitous in the 1920s, '30s, and '40s; millions were to be found in hotel rooms, lobbies, restaurants, bars, and the parlors and dining alcoves of American private homes. Parrish also illustrated books, advertisements, product booklets (for Jell-o Desserts), and calendars like those for Mazda Lamps. His paintings on canvas are now in the realm of high-priced art, but you can see his fantastic hand-painted fairy-tale murals in public places like the King Cole Room at the St. Regis Hotel in New York.

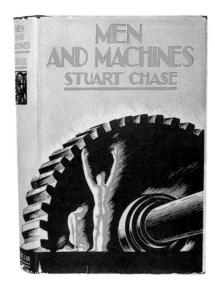

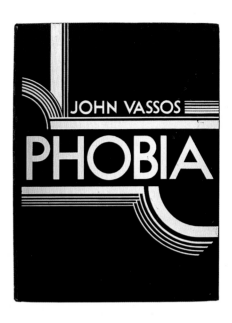

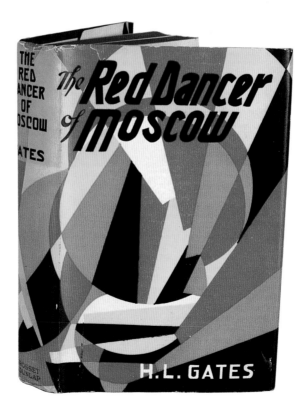

Men and Machines *by Stuart Chase. Hardcover book published by Macmillan, New York, 1929. Dust-jacket cover art by W. T. Murch.*

Phobia, *a book written and illustrated by John Vassos, published in a signed and numbered limited edition by Covice, Friede, Inc., New York, 1931.*

The Red Dancer of Moscow, *pulp novel by H. L. Gates, with Russian Constructivist Art Deco dust jacket, published by Barse & Co., New York and Newark, 1928, the basis for* The Red Dance, *a movie starring Dolores del Rio.*

"Modern Bread" wax paper wrapper, ca. 1930.

Maxfield Parrish cover illustration for Jell-o promotional booklet, copyright by the Genesee Pure Food Co., Leroy, New York, 1924.

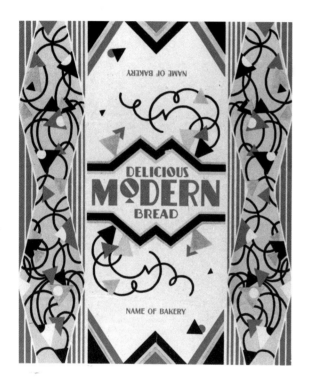

J. C. Leyendecker image lithographed on cardboard box for Arrow Handkerchiefs, 1931.

"Skyscraper Dance" by John Vassos, from a series of dance interpretation drawings. The Dance magazine, October 1930.

Yearbook for the University of Cincinnati, 1934.

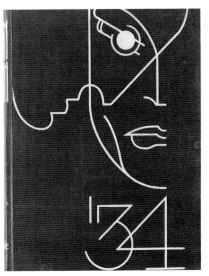

Murals by the famed Hungarian artist Willy Pogany depicting Jack and the Beanstalk and the Greek god Pan have been part of a children's theater at 1 East 104th Street in New York for sixty years and were recently rescued by concerned citizens when the theater was being restored. Murals by Pogany also lined the walls of the grand lobby entranceway of the Stanley movie palace in downtown Jersey City, New Jersey. Pogany, a member of England's Royal Society of Illustrators, painted in the pre-Raphaelite tradition, and in his American illustrations and murals conveyed a similarity in mood and style to Maxfield Parrish.

N. C. Wyeth created the art for more than 3,000 advertisements and also illustrated twenty-five books. Coles Phillips and Al Parker painted beautiful Art Deco women for *Good Housekeeping* and *Ladies Home Journal*, as did Harrison Fisher and Bradshaw Crandall for *Cosmopolitan*. Joseph Christian Leyendecker's illustrations for Arrow Shirts or Chesterfield cigarettes are high-style realistic portraits that have come to symbolize the Deco period for the many who admire and collect them. Other famous illustrators like James Montgomery Flagg or Norman Rockwell represented the indomitable spirit of Americanism through changing times, each in his own inimitable, highly original, and easily identifiable manner. Magazine ads, covers, or prints by these artists are now avidly collected, framed, and used as nostalgic decoratives for the home.

John Held, Jr., is renowned for his roaring twenties–Jazz-baby-flapper comic-style illustrations found in magazines, on posters, and on book jackets. Deco illustrators like Erté, George Lepape, Eduardo Garcia Benito, George Barbier, Louis Icart, William Welsh, René Vincent, D'Arcy, and others are sought after for their great stylistic flare and originality whether the artwork is original, a lithograph, or a magazine cover.

Surrealist-style Deco playing card.

Geometric-style Deco playing card.

Playing card with French-style floral Deco design.

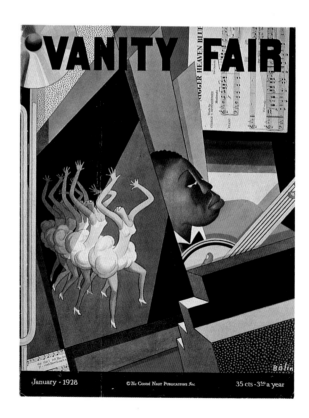

Vanity Fair, *January 1928, cover by Bolin, Condé Nast Publications, Inc.*

Jean Dupas, A. Mouron Cassandre, M. Ponty, M. Sironi, A. Zuthoff, Michel Bouchand, F. Ribas, Paul Colin, Otto Ottler, and Joseph Binder designed travel, product, and sales posters that are first-rate examples of high-quality lithographic or applied printing techniques in the modern Art Deco style.

Such magazines as *Vanity Fair* (which ceased publication in 1936 and began again in 1983), *Vogue*, *Harper's Bazaar*, *Fortune*, *Esquire*, *Life* (the pre-1936 humour magazine), *Woman's Home Companion*, *Cosmopolitan*, *Good Housekeeping*, *House Beautiful*, *House and Garden*, *Ladies Home Journal*, *McCall's*, *Modern Priscilla*, the *New Yorker*, *Arts & Decoration*, *Asia*, *Delineator*, *The Country Gentleman*, *Judge*, *Ken*, *Motor*, *Stage*, *Bachelor*, and *Theatre* all featured fine Deco covers and interior illustrations. Photographic styles and the photographic essay took on new meaning with magazines like *Life* and *Look*, which began to tell their stories through photo layouts like a Movietone newsreel. Fashion and product advertisements helped to create and perfect the age of photography, which was an important development of the machine age. Debates as to whether photos were to be considered art persisted in the 1930s, but with the brilliant work of photographers like Margaret Bourke-White, Walker Evans, Minor White, Imogen Cunningham, Henri Cartier-Bresson, André Kertész, Paul Outerbridge, Alfred Stieglitz, Edward Weston, and Paul Strand at the forefront of photojournalism it became increasingly difficult to argue the matter. Prominent among commercial photographers in the 1930s was W. Grancel Fitz, who pioneered photographic product enhancement geared toward consumerism.

The days of fine printing and quality paper stock, as espoused by periodicals like *Westvaco Inspirations for Printers*, a leading illustrated trade publication, entered a decline with the advent of World War II. Scrap

Lucky Strike Green modern cigarette packaging prototypes from the Raymond Loewy Collection. In 1940 Loewy redesigned the cigarette package (shown here), with the design innovation an exact "cleanlined" repeat image of the famous red bull's-eye target on both sides of the product. A classic example of streamlining in packaging; the one on the right made it into the tobacco stores.

Bridge tally card showing a 1920s flapper and tuxedoed gent, illustrated by John Held, Jr., ca. 1926.

paper Victory drives were the order of the day, and cheap wood-pulp paper was introduced for books and magazines.

In the *Seventh Annual of Advertising Art*, a published album of ads shown at the Exhibition of the Art Director's Club in 1928, the well-known advertising firm of Lord & Thomas and Logan in a declaration entitled "The New Spirit" stated:

Some of us attached to it the label "modern" . . . others avowedly know no name for it . . . we realize only that manifestations are everywhere—in art, in writing, in music, in furniture, in architecture, in industrialism—new forms, new lines, new uses of color.

In our craft it finds eloquent expression—it has become a force, unleashing imagination, unfettering creative ideas—employing for its purpose the highest form of advertising art, typography and copy.

Our fingers are sensitive to the pulse of our times—our eyes are forward looking—to newer spirits . . . to the things that arrest and awaken attention—AND QUICKEN THE ADVERTISER'S PROFIT.

In 1929, Westvaco conducted a survey of the advertising in two major magazines. Discovering that 250 out of over 400 advertisements showed modernism or had modernistic tendencies in illustration, layout, copy, or typography, they noted in their report that page after page in booklets, folders, and magazine advertising showed the influence of the "modern spirit." The conclusion drawn from this was: "From the instances cited, it would appear that within a short time all advertising will show the effects of this new modernistic school—a school that offers vast opportunity to the ingenious designer and printer who is equipped and ready to take advantage of it."

Deco gift box, paper lithography in silver and black on cardboard, 1930s.

Deco nude-nymphets set against a sunburst design, label for the 78rpm recording of "When I'm Looking at You" played by Vincent Lopez and his Orchestra, Perfect Record Company, 1930. Perfect Records, dime store subsidiary of Brunswick Records, featured artists like Ruth Etting and Cab Calloway. The Perfect label (which sold for 10¢, as opposed to better labels' top price of 35¢) existed from 1922 to 1937, promoting the fabulous music of the Deco era.

Holiday Deco

Christmas and Easter, two of the most important holidays of the year, were traditionally celebrated in an old-fashioned manner, but during the 1920s and '30s elements of modernity and the Art Deco style entered the picture in graphic designs for greeting cards, gift-wrapping paper, and gift boxes, as well as in holiday advertisements in magazines and newspapers of the day. Halloween and St. Valentine's Day also sometimes entered into the spirit of modernity, with one traditionally geared toward the darker side of ghosts, goblins, and witches and the other all cupids, hearts, and flowers. While Valentine's Day cards were often comic in spirit, there were many that were more serious and invoked the Deco spirit by featuring Erté-like ladies and dapper gentlemen in tuxedoes offering their sweethearts a heart-shaped box of chocolate candy.

Elongated geometric-style images of Santa Claus, snowmen, stylized leaping reindeer, and Scottie dogs frequently turned up to brighten the Christmas season during the Depression years. Though most of these holiday graphics came out of commercial art, they were often quite striking in terms of Deco, and in terms of the way a new chic sophistication joined otherwise-traditional celebration and merrymaking.

Delineator *magazine, December 1931, cover design by Dynevor Rhys.*

Moderne angel design by Rockwell Kent on 1939 Christmas seal for tuberculosis—"Protect your home from T.B."

Handsome Christmas card from the Depression era designed by "Volland Co.—U.S.A."

The Small Home *magazine, December 1930, cover design by Everett C. McNear, published by Architects Small House Service Bureau, Inc.*

Decorative lithograph-on-cardboard Christmas lingerie gift box with poinsettia and Art Deco geometric patterns, ca. 1930s.

Christmas greeting card featuring Scottish terrier waiting for Santa Claus at the window, ca. 1938.

MAY your holidays be just as happy as they were in the days you did believe in Santa Claus.

·· DECEMBER ··

SUN	MON	TUE	WED	THU	FRI	SAT
·	·	·	1	2	3	4
5	6	7	8	9	10	11
12	13	14	15	16	17	18
19	20	21	22	23	24	25
26	27	28	29	30	31	·

LASKY COMPANY, INC.
220 Elizabeth Avenue   Bigelow 2-2411   Newark, N. J.

Christmas greetings in the Depression from the Lasky Co., Inc., of Newark, New Jersey.

Cheerio Christmas greeting card, ca. 1934.

Depression-era lithographed-cardboard Christmas box for small objects or jewelry.

Plum Pudding? may I scrape the dish Minnie?

Christmas gift-wrapping paper illustrates six different "at home" holiday scenes. This one shows Mickey and Minnie Mouse in their Depression kitchen making plum pudding. Marked Walt Disney Ent., and produced by the Dennison Mfg. Co. of Framingham, Massachusetts, for the 1933 Christmas season.

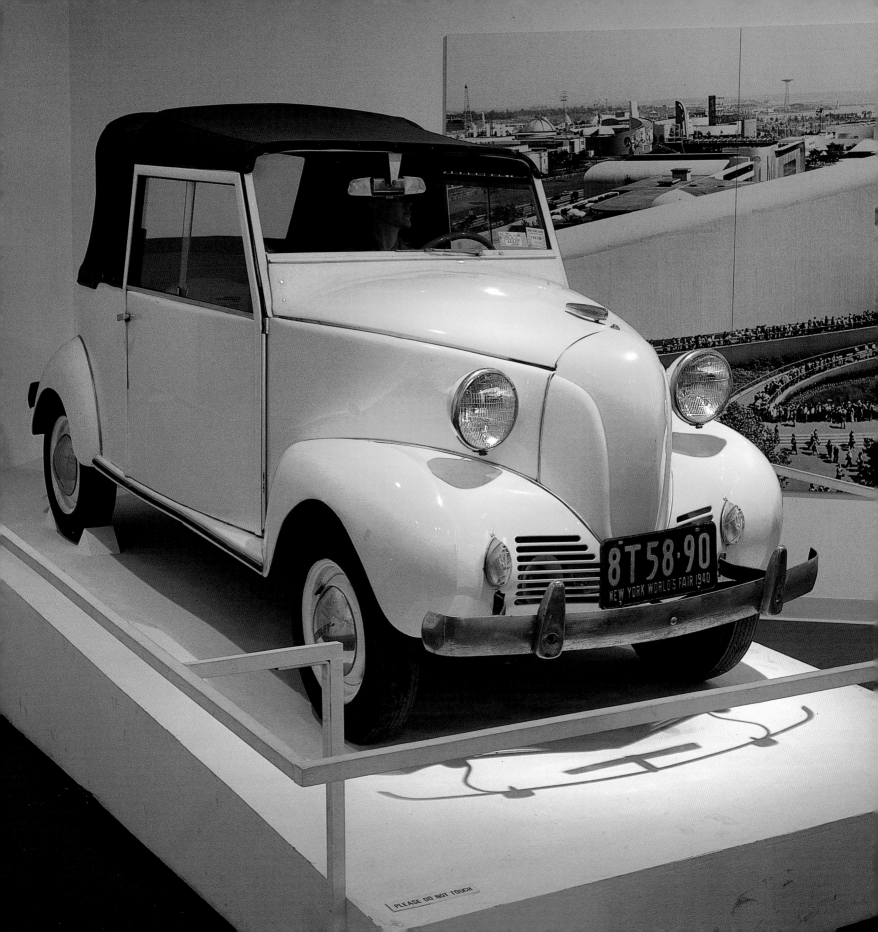

PLEASE DO NOT TOUCH

THE SHAPE OF SPEED

Aerodynamic and hydrodynamic principles suggested the streamlined teardrop shape as ideal for airplane, train, and automobile bodies, where least resistance is an important factor in achieving and maintaining speed. The streamlining concept was already apparent in the shapes of flying insects like ladybugs or Japanese beetles; and birds in flight and darting fish were the inspiration for some of the earliest studies of streamlining.

When they were first seen, the immense, silver, bullet-shaped rigid airships known as dirigibles and zeppelins were regarded as spectacles of streamlined splendor and beauty. Today such airships are used primarily as floating weather-detectors and billboards for advertising, but in the 1920s and '30s they were vehicles for a novel and exhilarating form of passenger air travel. Unfortunately, this mode of transport came to an end following the disasters of the U.S.S. *Akron*, which in 1933 plunged into the ocean near Barnegat Lighthouse, New Jersey, killing seventy-four

people; the lighter-than-air *Macon*, which in 1935 fell off Point Sur, California; and Germany's *Hindenburg*, with a full dance floor among its luxury accommodations, which burst into flame on May 6, 1937, at Lakehurst, New Jersey. Airships still traversing the skies, like the luxurious *Graf Zeppelin LZ 126*, were ultimately grounded after public outcry over their safety.

Buckminster Fuller, inspired by new advances in modern technology, developed his "Dymaxion" principle and created the Geodesic Dome, a unit of space that combined a maximum of floor space and a minimum of outer structural weight. In 1927 this renowned experimentalist, engineer, architect, and industrial designer created his Dymaxion House and invented a "4-D Zoomobile," which was an auto-air vehicle that could lift off the roadway and zoom into the sky. Unfortunately, the Zoomobile was thought to be both impractical and unsafe by manufacturers. Nevertheless, it was the forerunner in design concept

Crosley coupe convertible, 1941. This $325 two-cylinder midget auto was on view at the exhibition "Dawn of a New Day, the New York World's Fair 1939/40," Queens Museum, June 21–November 30, 1980. (Lent by Harold Serva)

of Fuller's three-wheel Dymaxion car (1933–34), which employed airplane body construction methods and is a perfect example of the aerodynamic teardrop shape.

Among outstanding American production-line automobiles that led the way toward acceptance of a streamlined torpedo shape with slanted radiators, windshields, and involute wraparound fenders were the Hupmobile (1934) designed by Raymond Loewy, the Chrysler Airflows (1934–37) designed by Carl Breer, the Auburn, and Gordon Buehrig's Cord 810 (1936). The Airflow design was said to have been inspired by flights of wild geese, which form a "V" shape while flying. The designer applied this natural principle, which was already used in aircraft, to the building of a car. The Chrysler Airflow and the DeSoto Airflow, which were years ahead of the same company's more conventional, boxy "Airstream" models, were described in a period automotive brochure as "functionally correct for cleaving through the air stream." The interiors of the Airflows were provided with overstuffed seats on exposed bent tubular chromium frames similar to those used in early airplane interiors. Other assembly-line futuristic, streamlined automobiles included the 1934 LaSalle, the 1936 Lincoln Zephyr, the Lincoln

THE
VEEDOL-LUBRICATED
HINDENBURG
BEGINS A NEW CHAPTER IN AVIATION HISTORY

4200 hp. from four Diesels speed this "flying hotel" on its trans-oceanic flights. Diesel power marks a new era in lighter than air transportation. It not only gives more economical power to the Hindenburg but permits higher speeds and greater safety. In fact, safety is promoted to such a degree that smoking is permitted.

Safety for the Diesels, from which smooth flowing power is vital, is assigned to Veedol. For more than 1,000,000 air miles Veedol has protected the power

of the Graf Zeppelin. Its performance has been proven beyond dispute. Quite logical that this finest of Pennsylvania oils should be assigned to safe-guard the performance of this 4200 hp. plant of the Hindenburg.

Take a lesson from the Zeppelins. The next time you need oil for your crankcase have it filled with Veedol. Give your automobile Zeppelin lubrication protection. Bear in mind that nothing is so expensive as ordinary oil, nothing more economical than Veedol.

VEEDOL MOTOR OIL
VEEDOL
THE HEAT-RESISTING FILM OF PROTECTION
MOTOR OIL AT ITS FINEST
TIDE WATER OIL COMPANY . . . 17 BATTERY PLACE . . . NEW YORK CITY

This smoking lounge on the Hindenburg was the only place where smoking was permitted on the ship. The chrome furnishings were up-to-the-minute in style and also lightweight.

Veedol ad on back cover of souvenir booklet from the U.S. Naval Air Station, Lakehurst, New Jersey, 1936. The Hindenburg came to a fiery end at Lakehurst in 1937. Tide Water Oil Company.

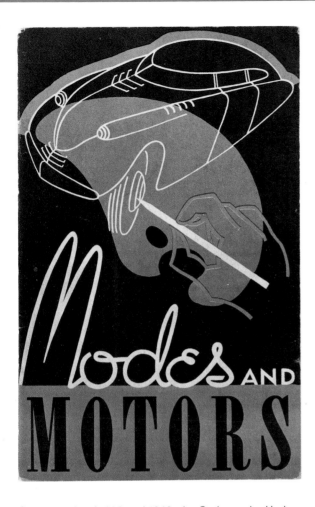

toward a truncated end. Millionaires like Phillip Wrigley invested in the Scarab and cajoled wealthy friends and business associates into owning one as a prestige status symbol. Appealing interior features included movable reclining rear chairs, a davenport couch, and a fold-up table. The hub of the steering wheel incorporated a stylized Art Deco image of a large, dark scarab in its center. The scarab beetle, a religious symbol of ancient Egypt, was also utilized on the hubcaps of this experimental automobile, of which only six appear to exist today. Experimental designs for cars sometimes included a large boat-tail in the center rear like that on the zippy convertible coupe driven by Roland Young in the film *Topper*. However, fin shapes did not becme really popular for automobiles until the 1950s, when they were added to rear-fender contours.

Modes and Motors, booklet cover by the styling section of General Motors Corp., published by GM in Detroit, Michigan, 1938.

The Shape of Speed: Raymond Loewy's S-1-style aerodynamic Streamliner train. Advertisement for the Maryland Casualty Co. of Baltimore, Maryland. Fortune, February 1938.

Continentals of 1939 and 1940, the Graham, the Hudson Terraplane, and, in a smaller class, the Willys and the Volkswagens of the 1930s.

Outstanding also in aerodynamic style was the short-lived Scarab designed by William Stout, which was unveiled in 1932. In 1935 Stout attempted to market a production-line model of Scarab to be sold for $5,000, a significant sum in the Depression. In the same year that this scarabaeus car appeared, Dr. Wunibald Kamm of Stuttgart proved mathematically that for speed the streamlined shape need not come to a sharp point. One of the Scarab's design features was that it did not end in a tear drop but tapered

"Unforeseen events . . . need not so often change and shape the course of man's affairs"

Budd Manufacturing Company, was also exhibited at the Chicago fair and was the first train to introduce a gleaming stainless steel exterior.

Raymond Loewy created advanced expression for train streamlining with his K4-S and S-1 locomotives made for the Pennsylvania Railroad. The S-1 model was an improvement over the K4-S, with a 6,000-horsepower engine and a steel sheet metal exterior.

The new luxury streamliners, which railroad magnates proudly built in the Depression era, included fully articulated private compartments, plush Deco-styled armchairs for maximum comfort, elegant full-service dining cars, open-view observation cars, and moderne-style cocktail lounges. Railroad advertisements were geared toward businessmen, movie stars, and "the correct people." The "20th Century Limited,"

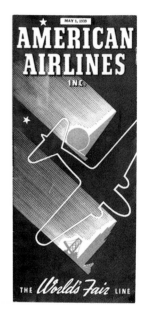

American Airlines timetable for travel between the Golden Gate Exposition of 1939 in San Francisco and the New York World's Fair of 1939.

The first high-speed streamliner train was the "City of Salina," which was designed in 1934 by Otto Kuhler for the Pullman Car Manufacturing Co., Inc. This lightweight train, enameled in sunshine yellow and earth brown, was egg-shaped on the engine front and to the rear. Called "Tomorrow's Train, Today!" by the Union Pacific Railroad, this stunning streamliner, with its chromium-steel modern interior and air conditioning, initially traveled on a "show stop" tour of twenty-two states before winding up at Chicago's Century of Progress World's Fair in 1933, where on exhibit it was viewed by over a million visitors. Its 12-cylinder 600-horsepower engine could propel the train at 110 mph. The Burlington "Zephyr," built by the

Streamliner train featured on the Little Orphan Annie's Secret Society 1940 membership booklet, a radio premium send-away from the makers of Ovaltine, published by the Wander Co., 180 N. Michigan Ave., Chicago, Illinois.

Wheaties "Breakfast of Champions" box, reverse side, showing diesel-powered, streamlined "Twin Zephyrs," ca. 1934.

THE NEW STREAMLINER "400" — CHICAGO AND NORTH WESTERN LINE

ULTRA-MODERN PARLOR CARS ON THE NEW "400"

9A-H1864

Ultramodern parlor car had seats that adjusted to any position; the new Streamliner "400," a Chicago and North Western Line train. Curt Teich "C. T. Art Colortone" postcard, Chicago, ca. 1938.

"The Super Chief," "The Blue Comet," "The Broadway Limited," "The Electroliner," "The Silver Meteor," "The Sunset Limited," and the "Hiawatha" were high-style modernistic trains that sped like thunderbolts across America in the great railroad years of the 1930s, offering glamour, comfort, and relaxation to their passengers.

In the early 1920s the whirring sound of a small plane traveling over a city's downtown area would find crowds gathering to gaze upward in awe and wonder at the new "daredevil" sport. Commercial passenger planes were in operation by 1928, but, because of the number of crashes, they were still regarded as dangerous by the public. No one seemed more heroic than pilots like Charles Lindbergh, who flew his single-engine plane, the "Spirit of St. Louis,"

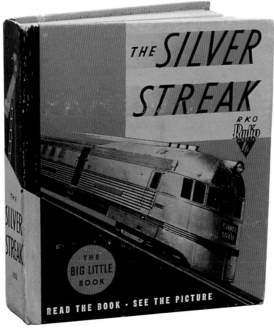

The Silver Streak Big Little Book is illustrated with scenes from the RKO Radio picture starring Sally Blane, Charles Starrett, Arthur Lake, and the Burlington "Zephyr." Copyright 1933 by Whitman Publishing Company, Racine, Wisconsin.

Uncle Don's radio premium giveaway booklet, 1936, from General Baking Co., featuring a fantasy aerodynamic scarab-shaped vehicle.

Centerfold illustration from Motor magazine, January 1935, with futuristic, electric streamlined vehicles that could travel on land, sea, or in the air.

William Stout's "Scarab," in the aerodynamic, streamlined teardrop style, was a production-line car in 1935 selling for the then high price of $5,000. Fortune, January 1941.

across the Atlantic in 1927; Rear Admiral Richard Byrd, who made his historic first flight over the South Pole in 1928; or Amelia Earhart, the first heroine of modern aviation, who made a solo flight across the Atlantic in 1932. In 1931 Pan American's Clipper ships, with their interiors furnished in a lightweight and casual Deco style, offered highly exciting flights to Rio and Buenos Aires from Miami, followed in 1936 and 1937 by the famed "China Clipper," which crossed 2,400 miles of the Pacific from San Francisco to Hawaii and then on to Hong Kong.

The real success of commercial aviation did not occur until 1937 when the twin-engine DC-3 appeared. It was then that Hollywood stars began switching to "overnight" coast-to-coast plane travel. As Ginger Rogers stated in a 1930s TWA ad, "On Transcontinental and Western Air you travel with the sort of people you enjoy meeting. You arrive fresh and rested." By 1940 a "silver bullet" whizzing through the sky was no longer an unusual sight, and the fast speeds of airplanes and their capability of traveling greater distances without stopping signaled the eventual decline in smart travel by train.

Exteriors of ships were also streamlined in the 1930s. The *Princess Anne*, a conventional ferryboat, was redesigned with rounded contours by Raymond Loewy in 1933 and launched in 1936; but it is particularly the splendid Art Deco ocean-liner interiors that come to mind today when we think of the *Normandie*, the *Queen Mary*, the *Ile de France*, and others. Leading European interior designers like Jules Leleu and Emile-Jacques Ruhlmann and American industrial designers like Loewy, Dreyfus, or Bel Geddes created lavish Art Deco furnishings and other special effects for these great floating hotels, which contained mammoth public dining areas, nightclubs, smoker–bar rooms, movie theaters, swimming pools, exercise rooms, kennels,

The 1935 Chrysler Airflow and Airstream cars. Motor *magazine, January 1935.*

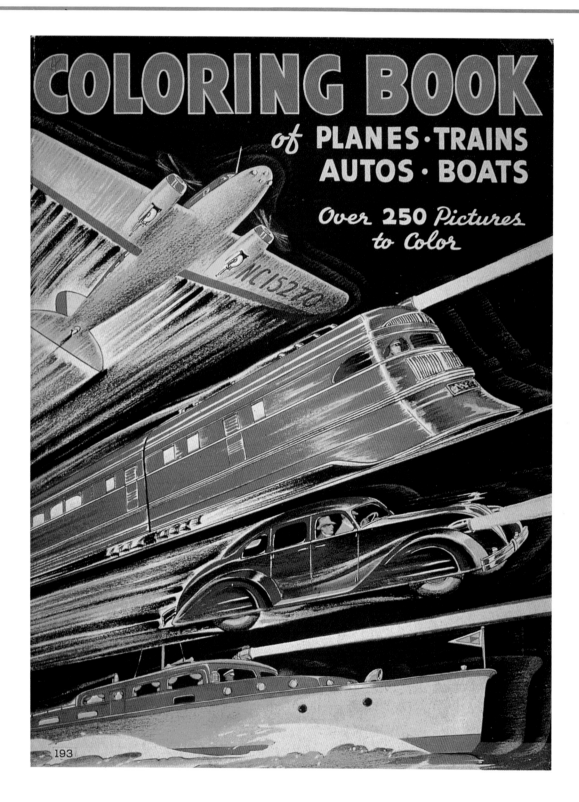

Coloring Book of "Stream-lined" Planes, Trains, Autos, Boats, *published by Rand McNally & Co., Chicago, 1936. The cover illustration is by Milo Winter.*

Mobil Gas Company's trademark, the flying red Deco-fantasy Pegasus, designed for the company in 1937 by Jim Nash, presented as an auto license-plate attachment, lithographed metal, 1940.

The Scarab interior offered passengers living room armchair comfort in the rear section, capacity six persons. William Stout rendering for interior, 1932.

CAPACITY: SIX PERSONS — WEIGHT 2100 LBS — HORSEPOWER 60 — TIRES 26×10 — WHEELBASE 130 INCHES.

DRIVE SAFELY

★ THE ★ CAR ★ OF ★ TOMORROW

AT THE WORLD OF TOMORROW

AS SHOWN AT THE CROSLEY BUILDING AT THE N. Y. WORLD'S FAIR ALSO THE AMAZING **FREEZORCOLD** Shelvador Refrigerator **Feather Touch Electric** MAGNETUNE RADIOS

SEE THE NEWEST OF THE NEW IN HOME APPLIANCES AT POPULAR PRICES

C R O S L E Y

Reado, facsimile radio printing—Crosley Camera, Press Jr. model—Gas and Electric Ranges — Electric and Gas Engine Washers — Electric Ironers — at Crosley Dealers everywhere.

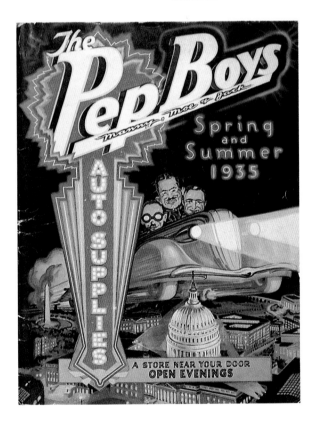

The Pep Boys *(Manny, Moe, and Jack) Auto Supplies catalog for spring and summer 1935.*

Souvenir postcard from the Crosley Building at the New York World's Fair of 1939, where the economical Crosley car, called "The Car of Tomorrow at the World of Tomorrow," was presented. The Crosley Co. also introduced the Shelvador Refrigerator,

the "feather-touch" electric "Magnetune" radio, the Crosley camera, electric ranges, washers, irons, and other newly designed appliances and products.

THE NEW STREAMLINER "400" — CHICAGO AND NORTH WESTERN LINE

THE NEW "400" OBSERVATION-LOUNGE CAR — SPEEDOMETER IN THE OBSERVATION SECTION SHOWN IN INSERT   9A-H1865

Colortone postcard of the Streamline Moderne lounge car of North Western Line Railroad's 400 Streamliner, Chicago to St. Paul and Minneapolis.

Greeting card with ocean liner and clouds and wave motifs in Moderne style, 1935.

Lighting sconce for interior of ocean liner SS Caribia.

Club car and cocktail lounge of the Burlington "Zephyr," in booklet from the Chicago, Burlington & Quincy Railroad Company, 1937.

Miles and minutes pass in a twinkling in the gay conviviality of the smart cocktail lounge

churches, nurseries, and fancy shoppes, as well as deluxe staterooms and suites.

Images of imposing luxury liners, sleek speeding trains, single- and twin-engine airplanes, amphibian planes, dirigibles, autogiros, and superfast automobiles were applied within the context of many original Deco designs, whether used in advertising graphics or as elements for architectural details, in lobby murals, or on modern vases, teapots, or novelty lamps or pieces of decorative statuary.

Norman Bel Geddes said in 1932, "Speed is the cry of our era; and even greater speeds are the goals of tomorrow." This optimistic view in the 1930s, put into practical application by industrial designers, created more of a public sense of trust for modern technology than had been entertained earlier in this century, when machines were often regarded with fear and apprehension.

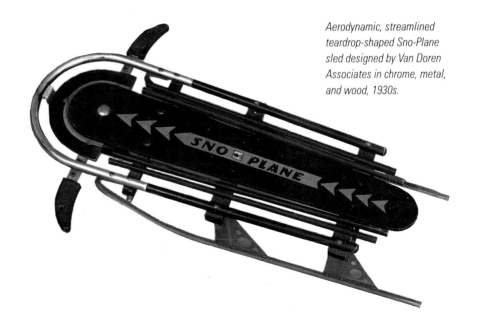

Aerodynamic, streamlined teardrop-shaped Sno-Plane sled designed by Van Doren Associates in chrome, metal, and wood, 1930s.

A CENTURY OF PROGRESS
EXPOSITION-1934
SEE CHICAGO
76
22
USE
CHICAGO SURFACE LINES
USE
CHICAGO SURFACE LINES

THE WORLD OF TOMORROW

The Early Fairs

In 1851 the first of the world's great industrial expositions was held in London in a gigantic steel-and-glass architectural wonder called the Crystal Palace. America's earliest "World's Fair" was held in New York in 1853 in a similar structure, also called the Crystal Palace. The next American fair, the Centennial Exposition of 1876, was sited in Philadelphia and became a prototype for subsequent world's fairs, featuring beautiful international pavilions. The largest and most successful world's fair of the nineteenth century was Chicago's Columbian Exposition of 1892–93, held to commemorate the 400th anniversary of the discovery of America. This fair was the first to introduce the postcard as a souvenir item.

One of the greatest fairs at the turn of the century was the Louisiana Centennial Exposition staged in St. Louis in 1905. The image of Napoleon—with whom the United States had negotiated the Louisiana Purchase in 1803—was used as the chief symbol on souvenir items. The St. Louis Fair was to be noted for its revolutionary electric light spectacle, and the breathtaking "turning-on" of the fair's lights was recaptured in the culminating sequence of the wonderful M-G-M motion picture *Meet Me in St. Louis*.

The Sesqui-Centennial International Exposition held in Philadelphia in 1926 adopted as its symbol the cracked Liberty Bell with the years "1776–1926" etched onto it. Though this fair was not considered economically successful, it did offer visitors an early glimpse of the growing thrust toward modernity: products of the Wiener Werkstätte, described in the official program as "modern fine art made in Vienna," were exhibited there. An "all-electric" eight-room house designed in 1920s Spanish Hacienda style with stucco exterior, wrought-iron balconies, and tiled rooftop featured many new electrical appliances and gadgets. These included a refrigerator, dishwasher, washing machine, an ironer, toaster, mixer, waffle iron, burglar

See Chicago—Use Chicago Surface Lines, travel guide booklet for the Century of Progress Exposition, 1934.

alarm devices, lawnmowers, and home heater units that were "*all electrified*." Foreign exhibits from more than twenty-five countries, including China, Japan, and Argentina, displayed native products and goods, and several state buildings were also prominent at this modest fair held the year following the landmark Paris exposition of 1925. The 200-foot-high Tower of Light Building, in the style of an Art Deco skyscraper, was lit at night with a display of revolving colored lights and a silver beam of light that made the building visible from many miles away. Souvenir merchandise from the Sesqui-Centennial included jewelry, ladies' compacts, and night lamps, all featuring an image of America's beloved relic—the Liberty Bell.

Powder compact, brass and enamel with inlaid rhinestones, souvenir of the Philadelphia Sesqui-Centennial of 1926.

Souvenir postcard of the "Tower of Light," Sesqui-Centennial International Exposition of 1926, Philadelphia.

TOWER OF LIGHT, SESQUI-CENTENNIAL INTERNATIONAL EXPOSITION.

PHILADELPHIA, PA.

THE ONLY BREAD BAKED AT THE CHICAGO WORLD'S FAIR

A Century of Progress

By 1930, after the arrival of the Great Depression, the idea of a utopian technological future was taking hold in America and would serve as the theme-format for all the startling visionary fairs to be held in that decade. The "Century of Progress" Exposition of 1933–34, with its symbol of a comet whirling through space, was held in Chicago on the shores of Lake Michigan and celebrated the 100th birthday of that city. The public was captivated by the futuristic Buck Rogers–style architecture and the magical lighting effects in color created by theatrical designer and architect Joseph Urban. Despite its being staged in the worst years of the Depression, the exposition was a financial success, with income chiefly derived from admissions and the rental of exhibition space.

At this Chicago fair, suddenly everything had become ultramodern; the concept of streamlining was applied to everything from household objects to automobiles and trains. The fair's architectural style, its buildings constructed with a view toward functionalism, was quickly labeled "Depression Moderne" by enthusiastic newspaper reporters.

The main proposition for the Chicago fair was "Advancement through Technology," and its central theme was "The Growth of Science and Industry," which was presented in detail at the Hall of Science.

General Motors, which used the expression "Who

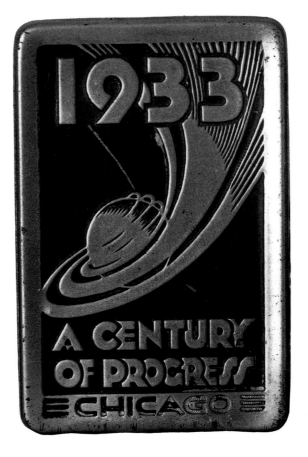

The Wonder Bread Bakery Exhibit, depicted on recipe booklet from Continental Baking Co., New York. Wonder Bread staged a popular exhibition at both the Chicago Fair (shown here) and at the 1939–40 New York World's Fair.

The Chicago Century of Progress Exposition swirling comet theme symbol, blue enamel on metal automobile license-plate attachment.

Serves Progress Serves America," built a modernistic 177-foot tower designed by Albert Kahn in which a visitor could choose the materials for a car, see it put together on the assembly line, and then drive it off completed.

Famous exhibition pavilions at the Century of Progress were the Travel-Transport Building, the Firestone Tire Building, the Sears, Roebuck Building, the Illinois Agricultural Building, and the Radio and Communications Building planned by famed architect Raymond Hood. The Electrical Building presented "The Miracle of Light," which consisted of neon tubes in a variety of intensely glowing colors. The Great Havoline Thermometer Building, which was 200 feet high, included, 3,000 feet of red neon tubing.

Notable in the modernistic style were the Glass Block Building, constructed by Owens-Illinois Glass Company entirely of many-colored semitransparent glass blocks; the Home Planning Hall, which showed beautiful modernist homes and featured a prefabricated seven-room Ferro Enamel House and a Florida Tropical House; and "The House of Tomorrow," a circular "air-cooled" glass house with sundecks, indirect "hidden source" artificial lighting, and also a private airplane hangar. Designed by George Fred Keck, it was built by Century Homes, Inc., of Chicago.

Foreign exhibits were from Italy, Great Britain, China, Japan, Denmark, Norway, Sweden, Czechoslovakia, Poland, the Ukraine, Morocco, Egypt, Mexico, the Dominican Republic, Belgium, and the Grand Duchy of Luxembourg. A Mayan temple and an edifice that incorporated a portion of the Great Wall of China were special attractions at this fair, and its Midway featured a Buck Rogers exhibit and exotic dancer Sally Rand clothed with just an ostrich-plume fan. If you were hungry you could eat "A BIG MEAL" at the Midget Village where Lilliputians were the cooks and

Enamel-on-chromium cigarette case in blue and white, the official colors of the Century of Progress–Chicago World's Fair, 1933.

Black-and-white lithographed illustration of the Electrical Building at Chicago's Century of Progress Exposition, from the hardcover booklet The Buildings of the Exhibition *by Franklin Booth, published by the Book and Print Guild, Winnetka, Illinois, 1934.*

the waiters. The adventurous could ride the twin tower cableway over the fair in a rocket car or take a whirl across Lake Michigan in the Goodyear blimp.

Chicago Today "The Magic
City of the Middle-West,"
tourist booklet showing 1930s
family watching futuristic television set. Drawing by
Kubricht.

Brilliant paper bumper sticker
advertising the Chicago Century of Progress Exposition,
copyright 1933 Howard M.
Rich.

Midwest, Southwest, and Western Fairs

The California Pacific Exposition of 1935 held in San Diego was meant to help stimulate economic recovery in California and the Southwest. In featuring Spanish Colonial and Baroque architecture, the fair made use of Mayan and Aztec decorative motifs that were often an integral part of Deco style. In 1936 both the Great Lakes Exposition in Cleveland and the Texas Centennial Exposition perpetuated the popular 1930s themes of modernism, technology, and progress toward a new and better world.

February 18, 1939, was the opening of the San Francisco–Golden Gate Exposition, ''The World's Fair of the West.'' Built on the 400-acre man-made Treasure Island in the middle of San Francisco Bay, the fair had as its main theme, ''culture and leisure.'' Its dramatic, towering, and imposing ''Pacifica'' architecture revealed a mysterious and alluring Far Eastern influence. At night the Court of Pacifica, the Court of the Moon, and the Court of the Seven Seas were spectacular wonders when bathed in spectrums of colored electric light. The Mines, Metals, and Machinery Building, which traced mining methods and the uses of metals from their earliest beginnings right up to the year 1999, was a highlight of the fair. The Electricity and Communication Building, presenting ''Modern Miracles in an Everyday World,'' featured television broadcasting from Radio Corporation of America and

Official Guide Book, *the Golden Gate International Exposition, San Francisco, California, 1939.*

a television receiving set from Westinghouse Electric and Manufacturing Company. Westinghouse also brought forth "Willie Vocalite," an electrical robot who at vocal commands could sit, rise, smoke, and, finally, speak. The Pacific Gas and Electric Company also had an "Electrical Man" who sang and told practical stories to bemused visitors. Among other attractions, the Hall of Science; the Ford Building, in which cars like the Lincoln Zephyr were assembled; agricultural displays; and international exhibits from a variety of countries were viewed by the throngs of people who came to Treasure Island to have fun.

The state of California—"Host to the World"—created a fiestalike atmosphere at this fair. There

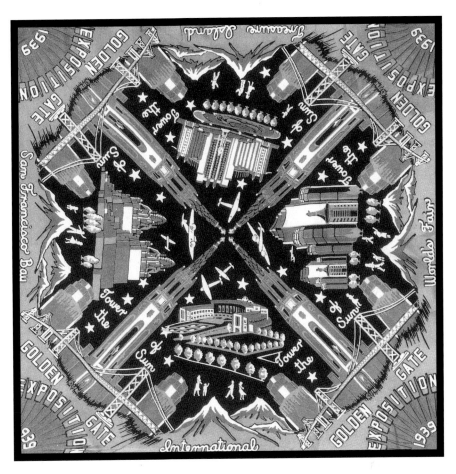

Rayon scarf, Golden Gate Exposition, San Francisco, California, 1939.

Official Souvenir Guide, Great Lakes Exposition, Cleveland, Ohio, 1936.

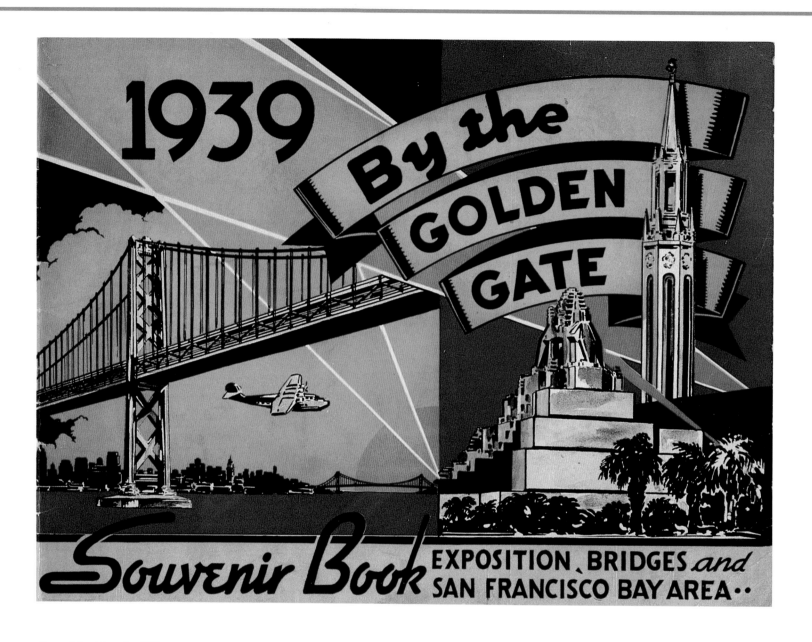

Souvenir book from the 1939 Golden Gate International Exposition, San Francisco. The Expo celebrated the completion of the San Francisco–Oakland Bay Bridge and the famed Golden Gate Bridge.

were, on the grounds, a California State Building and a San Francisco Building, both featuring historical dioramas; the Mission Trail Building, showing the missions of California and highlighting the popular "Mission style" in architecture; the Los Angeles–San Diego Counties Building; the San Joaquin Valley Building; the Alta California Building; the Sacramento–Tahoe Region Building; a Redwood Empire Building; and several others showing livestock and farm exhibits, Indian relics, goldmining, and sports events. Other states were represented, and the Territory of Hawaii sold holoku shell jewelry, monkeypod wood salad bowls, and floral-print rayon and silk Hawaiian shirts, skirts, bathing trunks, and kerchiefs.

By night the San Francisco World's Fair, celebrating the completion of the Golden Gate Bridge and the San Francisco–Oakland Bay Bridge, was a magical wonder. The brilliantly lit Elephant Towers and the Tower of the Sun, viewed from the cities and towns surrounding the San Francisco harbor, appeared to be bright glowing jewels when reflected in the dark waters of the bay.

On August 30, 1990, sixteen of the original twenty larger-than-life "Pacific Unity" sculptures from the San Francisco World's Fair were reinstalled by the Art Deco Society of California and the United States Navy in front of the Treasure Island Naval Museum Building, itself a survivor of the 1939–40 Golden Gate International Exposition. The sculptures included *Spirit of the Orient*, a cast-concrete statue by Jacques Schnier; an eight-foot-high, ten-ton sculpture of a Polynesian man; and figures of an Alaskan fisherman, a Chinese musician, and a Native American woman. The sculptures, a fountain, and a terra-cotta relief map of the Pacific region, created by nine California artists, had been in storage since Word War II.

Matchbook from the 1936 Texas Centennial Exposition showing the Petroleum Products Building, copyright 1936 The Diamond Match Company.

Official Souvenir Guide *for the Texas Centennial Exposition, Dallas, 1936.*

New York World's Fair of 1939–40

The most fantastic, futuristic, and influential fair of the 1930s (and of the twentieth century thus far) was the New York World's Fair of 1939–40 built on a 1,267-acre site in Flushing Meadows, Queens. The wonders of this exposition and the fully realized, functional, pop-moderne architecture exemplified by the whiter-than-white Trylon and Perisphere, structural symbol for The World of Tomorrow, continue to inspire the world of today more than fifty years later. As a blueprint for progress made in the past, the 1939 fair, built to celebrate the 150th anniversary of the inauguration of George Washington, still haunts us in the present day. It will certainly affect future generations to come with its vivid visions of a utopian world where technology was meant to be fully in the service of and for the benefit of all who would inhabit it.

Called "The World's Greatest Showcase" and "The World of Tomorrow," the 1939 fair was born, not unlike the other fairs of the 1930s, out of a time of despair, economic depression, and a desperate need for fantasy that focused on a better future. This largest, most comprehensive of all fairs originally had its roots in Le Corbusier's vision of the Radiant City and in the Bauhaus. The World's Fair was divided into seven zones: amusement and entertainment, food, communications and business systems, community interests, production and distribution, transportation,

Trylon and Perisphere chrome-metal picture frame with postcard insert of the theme center, New York World's Fair, 1939.

and the International Zone. The layout of the fair, with streets radiating out of several plazas, was reminiscent of the plan devised by Charles L'Enfant for Washington, D.C.

The 700-foot Trylon, a slender obelisk that pointed toward the sky, and the 180-foot-diameter spherical Perisphere were designed by Wallace K. Harrison and J. André Fouilhoux, who had been among the architects to conceive and build Rockefeller Center. Seen by many to be the best trademark since Eiffel built his tower for the Paris Fair of 1889, these two interrelated symbols became ubiquitous in every context and association with the fair. The theme exhibit of the fair was a diorama inside the Perisphere called "Democracity." Designed by Henry Dreyfuss as a sprawling

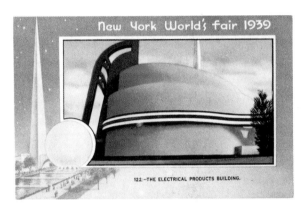

Three postcards from the New York World's Fair of 1939: Firestone Factory and Exhibition Building, Electrical Products Building, and Contemporary Arts Building.

Moderne-style Statue of Liberty with Trylon and Perisphere crown, painted by Witold Gordon, Vogue magazine, February 1, 1939.

Belgian wall tapestry, New York World's Fair, 1939. Left to right: Federal Building, Trylon and Perisphere Theme Building, Administration Building.

urban development imagined for the year 2039, this planned environment was meant to represent the ideal living complex. Democracity had tall apartment buildings and elevated, flowing highways that led to utopian suburban developments with artificial lakes, tree-lined streets, and with planned parks and recreational areas.

The spirited excursion to Democracity began with visitors riding up inside the Trylon on "two of the world's longest escalators," from which they were led outside again to an arched bridge that brought them into the Perisphere and onto two revolving platforms, one over the other. These platforms circled the interior of the sphere and offered panoramic views of the city below. After five minutes of viewing a perfect future, visitors were conveyed through automatic doors onto the "Helicine," a down-ramp exit.

The opening ceremonies on April 30, 1939, found Guy Lombardo and his Royal Canadians playing "Dawn of Tomorrow," written just for the occasion by George Gershwin. President Roosevelt addressed the public over an experimental television network of about 200 television receivers with nine-inch screens, all placed within a radius of about fifty miles. To assist in this first telecast by an American president, Eleanor Roosevelt was on hand, dressed in a sepia-colored silk dress dotted with small white Trylons and Perispheres. New York Mayor Fiorello La Guardia was also there on the opening day of what the *New York Herald Tribune* described as "the mightiest exposition ever conceived and built by man." At a cost of $155 million, the exposition would attract sixty million visitors who were anxious to believe what noted media expert Grover Whalen, the fair's president, had promised them: "This New York Fair will light the way to the advancement of human welfare and the betterment of mankind in every category of his existence."

Raymond Loewy designed "Transportation," one of the main exhibition buildings at the fair. A huge "light-up" map took visitors to various points of the globe by different modes of transport. Eventually a "rocketport" setup brought them into a "space-craft" that, following a radio countdown and a simulated rocket blast, took off for Mars. Loewy, who had gained fame as an industrial designer when he introduced his popular Coldspot refrigerator for Sears, also designed the Chrysler Exhibit, which followed the Bauhaus architectural dictum form follows function.

Numbered license-plate attachment, enamel on brass, for officials and executives of the New York World's Fair, 1939.

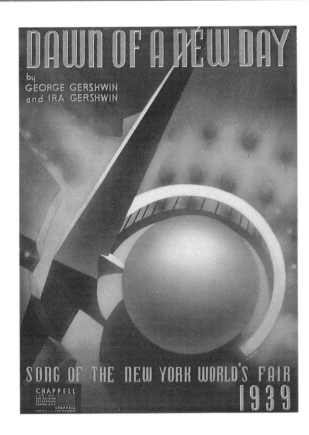

Sheet music for "Dawn of a New Day"; the "official" song of the New York World's Fair in 1939 was written by George and Ira Gershwin, prior to George's death in 1937, and published in 1938 by Chappell & Co., Inc., of Rockefeller Center, New York.

Porcelain-enamel and painted-wood kitchen table and four chairs decorated with Trylons and Perispheres. Detail on porcelain-enamel tabletop shows the Trylon and Perisphere in the official orange and blue colors of the 1939–40 New York World's Fair. Exhibited at Queens Museum, 1980. (Lent by the authors.)

Alladin's lamp–style ceramic teapot, New York World's Fair, 1939, a fair-licensed product made in Japan.

Just next door to the imposing Chrysler exhibition building was the Ford exhibit designed by Walter Dorwin Teague, who was often referred to as the Dean of Industrial Designers. Visitors could "drive" at the wheel of a 1939 or 1940 Ford on a conveyor belt that took them on a half-mile ride on the highway of the future. Teague, who had created a masterpiece of functional design for the Ford building, had also been influential in getting the fair's design board to incorporate his own obsession with a futuristic utopia into the overall concept of the fair. For Dupont he designed a modernistic tower; for National Cash Register a building that was an exact replica of a cash register, which "rang-up" the day-to-day count of fair visitors; for United States Steel a steel-structured dome with exterior girders to complement a feeling of open space within. Teague also created huge color blowups for Eastman Kodak to help introduce Kodachrome color film to the public. For Consolidated Edison, this indefatigable designer contributed to a huge diorama housed in a building three stories high and the length of a full city block. The animated scale model showed a full day's use of electricity in New York City, ending with a violent "electric lightning" thunderstorm. Con Edison promised visitors that gas and electricity for the home would cost them only pennies a year in the "near" future.

The Futurama, designed for General Motors by Norman Bel Geddes on a seven-acre site at the fair's top cost for an exhibit of $7 million, took visitors on a fifteen-minute journey to the year 1960. In plush upholstered moving armchairs, they crossed America, from sea to shining sea, with dawn awakening in the East and night falling like a blanket over the blue Pacific. The vast 35,000-square-foot Futurama diorama had 10,000 scale-model aerodynamic autos supposedly speeding at 100 mph on fourteen-lane superhigh-

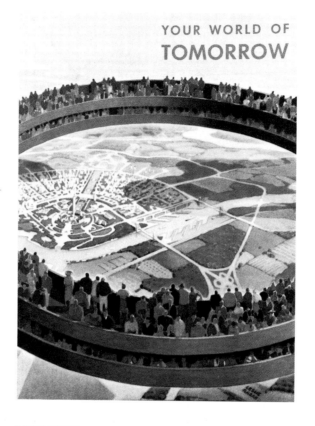

YOUR WORLD OF **TOMORROW**

View of the World of Tomorrow's "Democracity" inside the Perisphere, designed by Henry Dreyfuss. Souvenir booklet cover illustration by Leslie Sagan, text by Gilbert Seldes.

National Cash Register Building showing the world's largest cash register, which marked daily attendance at the New York World's Fair. (Courtesy of Larry Zim's World's Fair collection)

ways linking futuristic cities to the outlying planned suburbs.

Though both "Democracity" and "Futurama" were marvels of the model-maker's art, it was General Motor's "Futurama" that was the most popular, unforgettable, and dynamic exhibit at this fair.

The immense New York World's Fair of 1939 has sometimes been likened in yearning, spirit, and imagination to the wonderful Emerald City of Oz as depicted in M-G-M's classic film *The Wizard of Oz*, which was shown at movie houses that very same year. Dorothy, the Scarecrow, the Tinman, and the Cowardly Lion all wanted to get to Oz where their dreams could come true and where just about anything was said to be possible. *All* roads led to the fair—and an idealized future—in 1939 and 1940, just as a magical yellow brick road led to Oz. Each night at 9 o'clock, spectacular "technicolor" light shows called "The Ballet of Fountains," with great geyserlike water fountains and blazing fireworks, splashed over the Lagoon of Nations to the delight and amazement of the assembled crowds. Although sixty national pavilions ringed the Court of Peace, Germany was absent; Hitler had referred to the New York World's Fair of 1939 as modernistic nonsense. The Japanese Pavilion, which was a traditional Buddhist temple, showed off fine silks and art products with no hint that bombs and planes were also being manufactured in that country, soon to devastate Pearl Harbor and push America into a war in the Pacific. The spokesmen for the Polish Pavilion, who invited visitors "to holiday in gay wonderful colorful Poland," could not have known that the Nazis would invade their land during the run of the fair.

Pop oddities at the fair, other than Teague's giant cash register, included a Coty Pavilion shaped like a powder box and a giant Underwood Master Type-

"The Dream of the Radiant City," from an advertisement for Household Finance Corporation, Fortune, January 1932.

Giant-size souvenir matchbook, New York World's Fair, 1939.

writer reported to be the world's largest. The typewriter weighed 14 tons with each typewriter key weighing in at 45 pounds. It typed letters on giant 9-by-12-foot stationery, and the typewriter ribbon was 100 feet long and five inches wide.

The eight-story Railroads on Parade Building, which demonstrated the systems and capabilities of trains, past, present, and future, was one of the most popular exhibits at the fair. On display was the huge Raymond Loewy streamlined locomotive "K4-S."

Food exhibits were prominent at this whirlwind fair, referred to as "the most gastronomical," and included Borden's Dairy World featuring the Borden trademark Elsie the Cow, along with her pal Elmer the Bull. The Wonder Bread Bakery Building presented the wonders of new baking and packaging. At the Heinz Dome, after receiving a green plastic pickle pin (the fair's most popular souvenir), visitors were lectured to by a larger-than-life-size animated "Aristocratic" Red-Ripe Tomato Man in top hat and tails who also sang merry

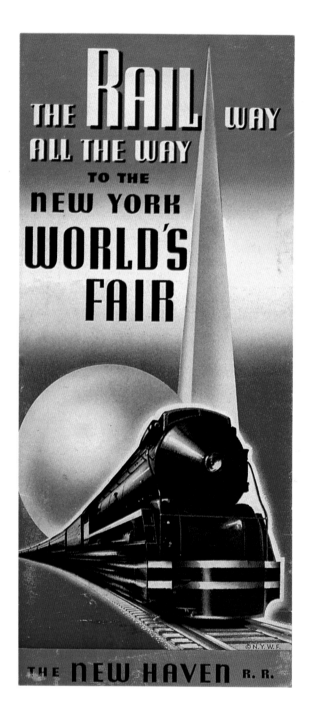

New Haven Railroad World's Fair souvenir booklet depicting Raymond Loewy's streamlined engine juxtaposed against the Trylon and Perisphere.

F. W. Woolworth & Co.'s dime stores, which were billed as "the headquarters for World's Fair souvenirs at hometown prices," gave their customers this complimentary map of the New York World's Fair, which included as well a rapid transit map of the New York subway system.

The aristocratic "Red-Ripe" Tomato Man, a synthetic rubber souvenir from the H. J. Heinz Company's Heinz Dome, New York World's Fair, 1939.

jingles about Heinz's "57 Varieties" of canned foods—oven-baked beans, "home-style" soups, spaghetti, tomato juice, or jars of pickles and relish—all available at a sample counter served by attractive "Heinz Pickle Girls." Two huge doughnut concessions operated by Mayflower, the Doughnut Casino and the Doughnut Palace, served delighted crowds crunchy crullers with Maxwell House "Good to the last drop" coffee.

The amusement-entertainment area's main attraction was Lifesaver's 250-foot-high Parachute Jump, which ultimately had a second wind at Coney Island. Eleanor Holm and Johnny Weissmuller starred in Billy Rose's *Aquacade*, a colorful "waterful" show spectacle. Whether you went to Frank Buck's "Jungleland"; Macy's "Toyland"; Phillip H. Lord's "Crusade-Against-Crime" in the Gangbusters Building; Admiral Byrd's "Penguin Island"; the Savoy Dance Center with its Harlem jitterbugs; Salvador Dali's surrealistic environmental "Dream of Venus" *Living* Sculpture Show; or Morris Gest's Little Miracle Town, featuring seventy-six midgets living in a miniature world (another parallel to the Munchkins of Oz), there was plenty of fun to be had at the New York World's Fair.

If you were one of the forty typical American families who were lucky contest winners, you might have been able to stay right on the fairgrounds at the two-model "Dream House," erected to FHA standards, for a full week's vacation. The World's Fair amusement area in particular became a prototype for Disneyland, Disney World, Great Adventure, and other family-style entertainment meccas of our own era. Disney's Epcot Center in Florida bases its format on the planned international pavilions, restaurants, and futuristic concepts of the 1930s fairs.

The Miracle of Glass, *Glass Center booklet, New York World's Fair, 1939, copyright Glass, Inc.*

Living room all in glass, featuring glass-brick windows, glass cocktail table, and fiber-glass fabrics. From The Miracle of Glass, *Glass Center booklet, New York World's Fair, 1939.*

Deco Souvenirs

No other single event produced more souvenir merchandise than the New York World's Fair of 1939–40. Nine hundred manufacturers were licensed by the Fair Corporation on a royalty basis to employ the image of the Trylon and Perisphere on more than 25,000 different items. Among these were pin-back buttons, hats, armbands, clothing, umbrellas, handkerchiefs, scarves,

ties, spoons, glassware, dish sets, teapots, salt and pepper shakers, commemorative plates, tumblers, dime store picture frames, vases, decorative statuary, ashtrays, compacts, wall plaques, novelty mood lamps, clocks, fine and junk jewelry, commemorative timepieces, money clips, furniture, an RCA Victor Syrocowood "Baby" radio, card tables, posters, flags and banners, employee badges and identification cards, guidebooks, magazines, playing cards, cookbooks, coloring books, comics, maps, merchandise and manufacturing booklets, postcards, paintings, prints, and souvenir menus.

Color-tinted photographic fabric design used for draperies, shirts, and dresses, New York World's Fair, 1939.

Frosted-glass table mood lamp with Trylon and Perisphere combined with bubble/cloud motif, 1939.

The Trylon and Perisphere in bright blue and orange —the official colors of the fair and of New York State—was a symbol of modernity and a new future, concepts that were certainly in great evidence during 1939 and 1940. Today, as testament to an important event of the machine age and modernism, memorabilia of this fair is collected with fervor both by World's Fair enthusiasts and avid collectors of Art Deco. Souvenir merchandise from Chicago's Century of Progress, 1933–34, and San Francisco's Golden Gate International Exposition of 1939, though not produced in such great quantity as the New York World's Fair, also fit easily into the World of Art Deco Fair Fever—the search for unusual fair objects that has become a new obsession. There is always something never seen before turning up with a Trylon and Perisphere on it, be it kitchen table, child's night light, eggbeater, or Bissell carpet sweeper. Then there are also the earliest television sets shown at the fair, among them the RCA TRK-12 designed by John Vassos, the small, efficient Crosley cars, and—it does not stop there!

A "time capsule" containing "A message from the year 1939 to the people of Earth 6939 A.D." was buried 50 feet deep on the New York World's Fair grounds. It contains millions of pages of information on microfilm and an interesting variety of modern objects, including an electric shaver and an Ingersoll Mickey Mouse watch. A similar time capsule was buried at the New York World's Fair of 1964–65 in Flushing Meadows Park, Queens, just yards away from the earlier one. Welcome to the Twilight Zone!

New York World's Fair water pitcher with blue "vitreous" decoration, Porcelier China, USA, 1939–40.

Embossed-leather souvenir wallet from the 1939 New York World's Fair.

1939 New York World's Fair lithographed paper bag.

THE WONDER CITY THEME

The skyscraper, regarded as America's main contribution to the advancement of modern architecture, reached unprecedented heights on Manhattan Island in the 1920s and '30s. In 1923 new "setback" resolutions were added to the New York Zoning Ordinance of 1916 to keep the city's streets from becoming a network of sunless and stifling caverns. These resolutions were important in determining the form for future skyscrapers by stipulating that they be "stepped back" from their bases as they moved skyward.

Manhattan's famed towers of commerce quickly became in themselves a popular Art Deco theme, inspiring, among others, the noted designer Paul Frankl to create his striking wood-and-lacquer bookcases and other furniture pieces in a modern setback skyscraper style. In the late 1920s and early 1930s mass-produced lamps, decorative vases, and even post-Prohibition cocktail shakers took on the "stepped-back" indentations of city skyscrapers. The form and image of the early New York skyscraper may also be found in Art Deco poster graphics, book dust jacket designs, magazine covers, product advertisements, and on coffee, powder, and candy tins. The skyscraper theme also asserted itself on costume jewelry, perfume bottles, and radio hardware.

Interior and exterior decorative details and images found on Art Deco skyscrapers—including lightning bolts, zigzags, chevrons, wave patterns, pyramid shapes, sunburst motifs, sunflowers, zinnias, cabbage roses, giant ferns, palm trees, eagles, condors, puffed-up doves, turkeys, pigeons, leaping deer and gazelles, running greyhounds, speeding autos, planes, trains, ships, and airships, and Aztec, Mayan, and Egyptian influences, as well as geometrically stylized forms of humans and mythic Greek gods—are also found to have been fashioned into designs for ladies' compacts and cosmetics products, fabrics, wallpaper, and a variety of other product designs and decoratives.

New York: The Wonder City, *guidebook published by Manhattan Postcard Company, Inc., 1936.*

Wherever new design was called for, the skyscraper image was drawn upon over and over again. Consequently, there was a dramatic interplay between environmental Art Deco images and architecture and mass-produced products, decoratives, and wearables. In the late 1920s and during the 1930s, the world was definitely Deco-mad.

Skyscraper *binding design, blue cloth over boards, published by John Day Co., New York.*

Pent House Chocolate Tid Bits, candy tin with skyscraper motif, Federal Tin Company of Baltimore, Maryland, lithograph on metal, ca. 1935.

Opposite: New York City's majestic Empire State Building by moonlight, shown with a dirigible moored to the mast atop the skyscraper.

A Deco Tour of New York City Skyscrapers

Just as in the 1930s, tourists from across the country and from all around the world still visit New York City in droves, to ogle the original, now landmark-status Deco skyscrapers built in just a nine-year period, from 1923 to 1932. Further construction was halted by the stringent new economics of the Great Depression. Completed in 1930, shortly after the stock market crash, the wondrous Chrysler Building at 42nd Street and Lexington Avenue, for a brief period the world's tallest building, highlighted the luxurious. William Van Alen, the chief architect, incorporated in his facade ornamentation stylized automotive symbols, including great winged radiator caps, giant eaglelike gargoyles, hubcaps, moderne trains, zeppelins, machinery parts, and other elements of the age of mass production and acceleration. A brilliant mosaic mural on the ceiling of the richly textured lobby depicts the building itself, while the apex of the building, composed of ascending scalloped half-circles and chevrons, is dazzlingly lighted.

Since 1931 the symbol of New York City and the cynosure of its skyline has been the Empire State Building at Fifth Avenue and 34th Street. The building was erected in only one year and forty-five days, and its anticipated construction costs were cut in half by the onset of the Depression to just $24 million. The architects, Shreve, Lamb, and Harmon Associates,

103:——EMPIRE STATE BUILDING BY MOONLIGHT. NEW YORK.

designed a base for the building five floors high. From a 60-foot setback at the fifth floor level, the building rises dramatically through additional setbacks on up to the 102nd floor. The slender television tower above (originally conceived as a mooring mast for dirigibles) makes the building soar to 1,454 feet.

Brilliantly illuminated in modern times by lighting wizard Douglas Leigh, the building was first officially "turned on" by President Herbert Hoover, who pressed a specially installed ceremonial button in the White House on May 1, 1931. The very top part of the building was not lit until November 1932, when a searchlight beacon signaled to those in a 50-mile radius that Franklin Delano Roosevelt had been elected president.

"Immortalized" in 1933 in the film classic *King Kong*, starring Fay Wray and Robert Armstrong, the Empire State Building is perhaps the quintessential Art Deco landmark. It is to New York what the Eiffel Tower is to Paris: the main tourist attraction. A visit to the observation tower to view the panorama of Won-

The three exemplary Deco skyscrapers from the 1930s are (left to right): The Empire State Building, the RCA Building in Rockefeller Center, and the Chrysler Building. C. T. Art Colortone postcard, Curt Teich & Co., Inc., Chicago.

der City and surrounding areas for up to 80 miles on a clear day is an imperative for all who visit the Big Apple. Visitors, standing in the astounding Rose Famosa and Estrallante marble three-story lobby with its nickel and bronze Art Deco details, stare in fascination at a brass and aluminum relief mural of the building, itself fully three stories high. Today Art Deco enthusiasts avidly collect 1930s, '40s, and '50s souvenir merchandise of the Empire State Building, which includes a variety of ashtrays, paperweights, souvenir plates, sculptured metal bookends, thermometers, mood lamps, salt and pepper shakers, and other collectible ephemera such as postcards, guidebooks, special commemorative booklets, and the like—all emblazoned with its image. Indeed, it would be difficult to find a home in America that does not have some kind of artifact with the Empire State Building featured on it.

Rockefeller Center, now a landmark complex, occupies three large New York City blocks from 48th Street to 51st Street between Fifth and Sixth avenues. The

Dinner plate from a series called "Our America," this one depicting the Manhattan skyline, designed by Rockwell Kent for Vernon Kilns, ca. 1940. (Mood Indigo, Soho, New York City)

The pioneering New York Art Deco Society conducts many tours of Wonder City Art Deco skyscrapers that are certain to include the famed McGraw-Hill Building on West 42nd Street. Sheathed in multishades of green-blue terra-cotta, the McGraw-Hill headquarters was built in 1930–31 by André Fouilhoux in

ultimate, sparkling, well-lit, and radiant city-within-a-city unit consists of twelve highly decorated Deco buildings that include the 70-story RCA (now GE) Building at the top of which is the famous Deco Rainbow Room with its panoramic views of the Wonder City. Street-level entrances and plazas abound in Rockefeller Center, with mythic Greek figures and statuary groups of American tradesmen and laborers executed in terra-cotta, stone, cement, metal, frosted glass and crystal, and in stunning mosaic tile murals. The Radio City Music Hall itself, with its great stage, auditorium, grand foyer, and lounges designed and decorated by Donald Deskey, has gained official landmark status for its interiors.

collaboration with Hood and Godley. It is regarded today as a classic example of the Streamline Moderne style as applied to architecture. Also on 42nd Street, on the East Side, is the handsome Chanin Building, which uses exotic French Art Deco romantic floral exterior ornamentation. Designed by Sloan and Robertson, the Chanin theme of "City of Opportunity" incorporates aspects of work and industry into its design motifs and overall concept. Both the Daily News Building on East 42nd Street (1929–30) and the American Radiator Building at 40 West 40th Street (1923–24) were designed by Raymond Hood and would certainly be highlights of any sightseeing tour of "Deco City." Remarkably, these examples are just the tip of the iceberg of stunning Art Deco skyscrapers that add such a sense of wonder to the skyline of Manhattan.

The Hotel New Yorker, in its 1930s–'40s heyday as an Art Deco landmark, featured a private tunnel to Pennsylvania Station, 2,500 rooms, each with a radio, four restaurants, and the famous Art Deco Terrace Room. Johnny Roventini, the bellboy who became a living trademark for Philip Morris Cigarettes, began his career at this hotel. Rates in the 1930s started at $3.85 per day. Postcard E. C. Kropp Co., Milwaukee, Wisconsin.

Baggage sticker from the Hotel New Yorker, 34th Street at Eighth Avenue. Color lithograph and gold leaf on paper, ca. 1935.

Automatic Deco for a Nickel

New York City had its own restaurant chains like Riker's, Bickford's, Rudley's, Nedick's, the Waldorf Cafeterias, and Schraft's that were modernistic, sanitary, and efficient. However, it was the Automat chain that had to be the ultimate in quick, easy, mechanistic, and nonobtrusive dining—they served the very best in home-style cooking. "Making It Easier for Mother" was the motto of Horn and Hardart's self-service Automats, the wonder restaurants with automated, coin-operated revolving food servers. Put a few nickels in a slot, turn a knob, and a little metal-and-glass compartment would pop open to reveal a sandwich, a piece of pie, a crock of oven-baked beans (with or without frankfurters), or other choice side dishes.

The first Automat restaurant opened on June 12, 1902, in Philadelphia. Operating only in New York City and Philadelphia, Automats served almost a million people a day throughout the 1920s, '30s, '40s, and '50s. In the 1960s the quality of the food suffered a decline, and by the 1970s, in association with increasing economic problems, the novelty of the Automat seemed to have worn off. Today only one exemplary Automat still exists for regular business or special party rentals, at Third Avenue and 42nd Street. In the late 1980s the Horn and Hardart Company opened two restaurants that incorporated the gleaming chrome

Egyptian Moderne–style Automat on 57th Street, opened August 1938.

Horn & Hardart's one-pound Automat coffee tin (the coffee was said to be the most delicious in New York and was always served piping hot for just a nickel!).

and formica details of 1950s diners. Called Dine-O-Mats, they served abundant lunches and dinners and gigantic fountain specialties in a nostalgic and sparkling 1950s atmosphere complete with reproduction Wurlitzer jukeboxes and singing bobby-sox-clad waitresses. Both of the now defunct Dine-O-Mats, on Third Avenue at 57th Street and on University Place at Washington Square in Greenwich Village, attracted happy and hungry crowds even though the little glass-faced compartments were nowhere in evidence. To see an original Automat intact, one must travel to Washington, D.C., where an entire Automat is on display at the Smithsonian Institution as an important icon in America's heritage.

Many say it was the steady decline of the nickel that hurt Automats. A cup of coffee for a nickel had long been an Automat mainstay, so when economic necessity forced the price to a dime this seemed to affect the overall ''everyman'' concept of the chain. Joseph V. Horn and Frank Hardart, who first met in 1888, often stated their simple credo: ''The real trick is to sell a good item cheaply.'' Both partners continued to sample the day's menu for many years, to make certain the cooks were maintaining the high standards they had set for the Automat restaurants.

Visiting an Automat became a must in the Depression for Gotham tourists and celebrities alike. In the 1930s one might have found Jean Harlow, Jimmy Durante, Jack Benny, Walter Winchell, Ethel Merman, or other show-folk putting a buffalo nickel into a slot and pulling a lever to release from the mouth of a chromium dolphin-head spigot fine French-drip coffee (its formulation a well-kept company secret). In addition to the nickel-in-the-slot food, Automats served good, wholesome, well-rounded American meals like roast turkey, browned potatoes, and creamed corn. Pick-and-choose commissary style food was dished

out by friendly uniformed attendants from stainless-steel warming trays.

The most popular Automat was the two-story 46th Street Times Square location that allowed visitors to gaze out on the famous Wrigley's sign, said to be the largest in the world. Situated 75 feet above the low-lying roof of the International Casino nightclub and stretching an entire block, the neon aquatic scene incorporated rippling blue waves, glowing yellow fish, and multicolored bubbles that floated up to the trademark green Wrigley man fishing from a giant rowboat. The Planters Peanuts' animated Mr. Peanut neon and the Camel cigarettes sign that pictured a man who blew out actual giant-size smoke rings onto Times Square were for many years integral parts of Broadway's Great White Way.

Irving Berlin celebrated dining out on a few nickels in *Face the Music*, a 1932 Broadway show that found a chorus of society folk down on their luck due to Old

Automat neon sign on 23rd Street produces reflections in the rain.

Interior view of Horn & Hardart Cafeteria at 122 Pearl Street, New York, which shows bronze grilles and details. F. P. Platt & Bros., architects.

''Welcome New York World's Fair Visitors,'' Horn & Hardart Automat matchbook cover, 1939.

Horn & Hardart on 57th Street at Sixth Avenue. There were more than 150 Horn & Hardart Automat cafeterias, restaurants, and retail shops in New York and Philadelphia, serving over one-half million patrons a day. Lumatone Photoprint postcard.

Horn & Hardart Automat Cafeteria interior, 545 Fifth Avenue, with terra-cotta, tile pillars, and zigzag terrazzo floors.

Man Depression suddenly reduced to eating at Horn & Hardart's. Nevertheless, they cheerfully sang out ''Let's Have Another Cup of Coffee, Let's Have Another Piece of Pie'' on a stage-set replica of an Automat—and why not? It was considered the best place in town for a meal.

Automats thrived and multiplied in the Depression era, and many of them were designed as monumental Art Deco emporiums with bronze fittings, beveled mirrors, stained glass, mahogany wood paneling, glazed terra-cotta decoration, and marble walls, as well as great chandeliers, Deco wall sconces, and hidden recessed lighting—an environment that would cost a pretty penny today. A cup of coffee—or anything else—for a nickel is now nothing but a memory.

New Facades

Many small shops, shoe stores, ice-cream parlors, beauty salons, restaurants, and night spots in cities across America remodeled their exteriors in the newest moderne, streamlined styles after Depression economics curtailed major building projects. The Cushman Bakery chain went Streamline Moderne by adding cream color and blue trim "Veribrite" porcelain-enamel storefronts, while other nationwide store chains employed Formica frontal inlays, Vitrolite, or sheer Carrera glass in a variety of colors offset by glass blocks, Monel metal and chromium trim, tile, and flowing tubular neon lighting. These external and interior modernizations were a relatively inexpensive way of creating an exciting, uplifting change in the Depression years of Roosevelt's New Deal.

American "Dream" diners, fabricated from industrial designs on factory assembly lines, incorporated stainless steel, glass brick, tile, and outsize neon signs displaying the words "EAT" or "DINER" to attract highway motorists or city dwellers. On the inside, cobalt blue or peach mirror accents, attractive recessed lighting, and metal venetian blinds contributed to the desirable overall sanitary and streamlined effect.

The early Pop-Deco White Castle System hamburger chain ("Buy 'em by the Sack") opened its shiny white, black trimmed, porcelain-enamel miniature castle res-

WPA-style mural on Streamline Moderne Telegraph Hill apartment building in San Francisco, showing China Clippers flying above bare-chested figure holding a globe, with the Oakland Bay Bridge below. Mural created by Alfred du Pont, J. S. Malloch, architect. (Humphrey Bogart and Lauren Bacall lived here, and Dark Passage, a movie they made together, was filmed there in 1947.)

White Diamond chain restaurants were miniature black-and-white porcelain-enamel Deco castles, matchbook cover, ca. 1940.

Restroom sign in bronze metal, Verner's Restaurant, Baltimore.

Cover illustration by Charles DuBose on American Architect and Architecture magazine, June 1937, shows new, modernistic storefronts using colored Carrera glass and glass brick with chrome detail.

Streamlined industrial building employing glass bricks, General Vending Co., Baltimore, Maryland.

Art Deco booth in Verner's Restaurant, Baltimore, Maryland, with chrome, wood Formica, and Bakelite details.

taurants in 1921, ultimately serving square five-cent hamburgers packaged in cardboard castle containers, as well as piping-hot coffee (also a nickel), to millions of Americans. Derivations of the White Castle theme turned up in rural and urban areas and included chains like Toddle House, Hull Dobbs House, Blue Castle, White Diamond, White Clock, Red Beacon, White Tower, Coon-Chicken Inn, and Krystal, all employing uniformed help who served hot dogs, hamburgers, crullers, and coffee without fanfare and in a jiffy. Other popular early eatery chains included the bright-orange-enamel Stewart's Root Beer drive-in stands and the tangerine-tile-roof Howard Johnson's.

Glass-brick column lights up in the vestibule-stairwell of a Telegraph Hill apartment building at 1360 Montgomery Street, San Francisco. (Note scalloped Deco banister and streamlined radiator grill.)

Art Deco architectural details on "Painted Lady"–style house, Diamond Heights, San Francisco, California.

Leaping dolphin in silver-leafed plaster, decorative detail from Rincon Center (formerly Rincon Annex Post Office) at Mission and Spear streets, San Francisco, California.

Construction worker in cast cement, Pacific Gas & Electric Building, corner of Beale and Market streets, San Francisco, California, 1925.

Blue and silver terra-cotta building (formerly the Oakland Floral Depot, now a series of small shops owned by the Rouse Company) at 19th and Telegraph, Oakland, California.

Terra-cotta

Terra-cotta, which has been used since Roman times for architectural embellishment, was one of the most exciting, colorful, and decorative building materials employed during the periods of feverish construction in the 1920s and early 1930s. As building blocks of clay that either fit together to form a decorative pattern or as single ornamental pieces, terra-cotta (Latin for "baked earth") was found to be an extremely plastic material and a good substitute for more expensive granite or marble. In natural clay colors or tinted to complement other building materials, terra-cotta also came with combed and crinkled surfaces for textural variety, an innovation of the 1920s. Machine-extruded terra-cotta began to be manufactured in the 1930s for the new, flatter look of Art Deco.

Though polychrome glazing techniques were developed as early as the fifteenth century in Italy, colored terra-cotta did not become popular as a decorative material until the 1920s, when it was intended to stand out and attract attention in building lobbies and at street level on facades. Deco shades included colors like lime green, lavender, and ebony, and there were glazes in matte or glossy finishes in all varieties of yellow, green, blue, and metallic silver and gold. Leading architects began using colored and decorative terra-cotta to highlight cornices and setbacks on skyscrapers.

Terra-cotta zigzag and Streamline wave motif on the facade of an apartment building on East 22nd Street in New York City, 1928.

"Turkey Deco" terra-cotta panel on industrial building at Washington and Linden streets, Newark, New Jersey, ca. 1931.

Terra-cotta panel for the interior of the Atlantic City, New Jersey, bus station on Arctic Avenue, 1930.

The Northwestern Terra Cotta Company of Chicago, said to be the largest in the nation, had a 400-foot tunnel-kiln in which terra-cotta blocks inched along in train carloads for a week of slow baking. Tens of thousands of glaze formulas were available, with a wide range of intense color that went from the standard commercial buff to ceramic gold to aquamarine to royal red. The Northwestern company borrowed ready-made designs from Paris exposition catalogs, which saved on artists' fees. Popular design subjects included flowers, zigzags, plump birds, exotic dancing women, chevrons, lightning bolts, sunbursts, heads of gods and goddesses, bulls, rams, rabbits, and turkeys. Examples of all of these are found on buildings throughout America.

Raymond Hood used gold-luster terra-cotta detailing on the tower of the American Radiator Building and sheathed the McGraw-Hill Building completely in blue-green terra-cotta tile. During the 1930s both buildings were dramatically lighted to emphasize the reflective abilities of terra-cotta, a practice that was only revived in the 1980s. Once again terra-cotta–decorated buildings glow by day and night. A prominent example in New York is the Sloan and Robertson Chanin Building, which has decorative terra-cotta at street level and at its top.

Terra-cotta was used widely on hotels, garages, gas stations, banks, automobile showrooms, commercial stores, and countless other multipurpose buildings. Movie theaters incorporated decorative terra-cotta on both the exterior and interior. Thomas Lamb's Loew's Theater (1930) at Broadway and 175th Street in New York, now the home of Reverend Ike's United Church, is covered in white-glazed terra-cotta. WPA artists and muralists employed terra-cotta extensively, and it was used on many of the sculptures, fountains, and structures at the 1939 World's Fair. New York apartment buildings with remarkably decorative terra-cotta include George and Edward Blum's grand apart-

Terra-cotta ornamental detail featuring Art Deco puffed-up doves, sunburst, and triangular shapes. Near North Side, Chicago, Illinois, ca. 1930s.

ment complex at 235 East 22nd and another at 210 East 68th Street, built in 1928 and 1929 respectively. National retail companies, especially the chains, used terra-cotta to express their identities and individuality; Child's Restaurant, which specialized in serving seafood, employed images of Neptune, crabs, snails, and seahorses, in its terra-cotta decoration. Horn and Hardart's Automat sported stylized floral motifs and zigzags in a Deco mode. Kress, Woolworth, and A. S. Beck shoe stores used simple, streamlined, monochromatic, angular Deco-styled terra-cotta on retail outlets across America. Slated today as the cornerstone for redevelopment in downtown Oakland, California, is the brilliant midnight blue with silver terra-cotta trim Floral Depot Building, which originally housed Kress's, Western Union, and a mini-mall of other retail stores.

There was a decline in the use of terra-cotta in the late 1930s when modern architects began to prefer materials that were completely mass-produced by machine, like metal, glass, and cement, so decoration on buildings gave way to stark, clean lines.

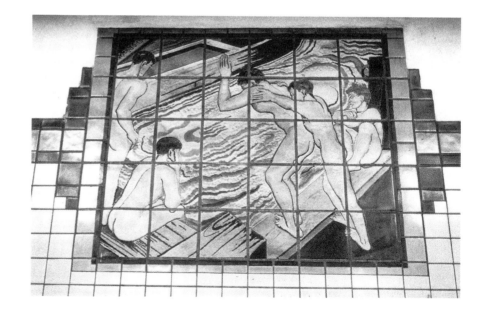

Tulsa Deco

Tulsa, Oklahoma, which had its beginnings as a Creek Indian trading post, began to be settled by white traders, adventurers, and cowboys by the 1880s. After the eventual discovery of oil, Tulsa was to describe itself in the 1920s as "The Oil Capital of the World." "Black gold" money flowed into the city during the jazzy twenties, and wealthy oilmen opened their big houses to all-night parties with heavy boozing and modern flappers doing the Charleston to wild Dixieland music. By 1927, as a way of showing off their easy money, hucksters like Waite Phillips, brother of the founder of the Phillips Petroleum Company, began to invest in the creation of a better downtown area for Tulsa; and they were attracted to the new ornamental style in architecture espoused at the Paris exposition of 1925. Deco in mind, the Tulsa of the madcap twenties tossed ideas of the stuffy old-style Gothic architecture out the window.

With an "easy come, easy go" oil-town attitude, reckless, extravagant, and daring men embraced the showy, colorful, whimsical style of Art Deco as they erected the towering monuments of Tulsa. Even today Tulsa exists as a bright oasis of commerce, culture, and fine Deco buildings set in the middle of the green hill-country of northeastern Oklahoma.

Basically, Tulsa Deco architecture can be divided into the Art Deco Zigzag Skyscraper style of the 1920s

Terra-cotta frieze above the entrance on the WPA-style Tulsa Fire Alarm Building, Tulsa, Oklahoma.

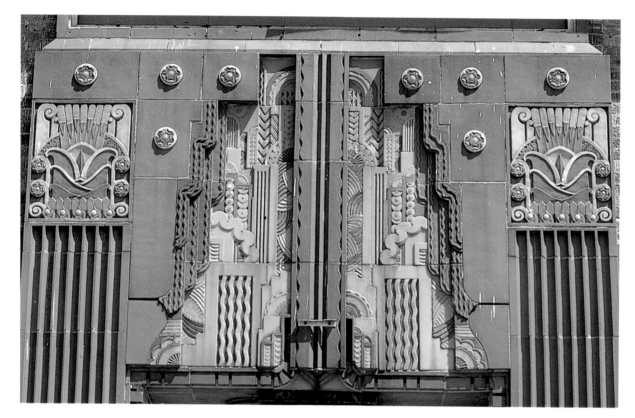

Jazzy terra-cotta ornamentation on Warehouse Market Building (now the Dollar Saver Discount Store), in Tulsa, Oklahoma.

and the PWA (built by the New Deal Public Works Administration) and Streamline Moderne styles of the 1930s. The 1920s Art Deco Zigzag style building was made possible by the use of light, durable, glazed and unglazed terra-cotta as sheathing material and for decoration. Zigzag incorporated chevrons, triangles, stepped platforms, fronds, and other jazzy Deco devices. Tulsa, because of its extensive use of brightly colored baked clay ornamentation on buildings, has been dubbed "Terra Cotta City" by Art Deco enthusiasts and landmark preservationist groups.

The chief architects of the Art Deco period in Tulsa were Barry Byrne, who designed the expressionistic, carved-limestone Christ the King Church in 1926, and Bruce Goff, who designed the Guaranty Laundry Building, the Midwest Equitable Meter Company, the Tulsa Club, Riverside Studio, the Merchant's Exhibit Building at the Tulsa fairgrounds, and the Boston Avenue Methodist Church, which looks like it was inspired by one of Hugh Ferris's fantasy tower drawings. The Frank Lloyd Wright influence is found in Tulsa in upper-middle-class suburban homes, notably the Richard Lloyd Jones House, "Westhope," built in 1929–30.

Other outstanding Tulsa Art Deco buildings (out of more than a hundred primary examples) include the black-glass-covered Security Federal Savings and Loan Building, the Medical and Dental Arts Building, the Oklahoma Natural Gas Building, the Public Service Building, the ten-story Bliss Hotel, the Halliburton-Abbott department store, the Gillette-Tyrell (Pythian) Building, the Tulsa Fire Alarm Building, the Southwestern Bell Main Dial Building, the Will Rogers High

School, the Will Rogers Theater, the Webster High School, the Tulsa Union Depot (recycled in 1983 as an Art Deco office complex), and the Philcade, built by Smith & Sentes in 1930 for oil baron Waite Phillips as a sister building to his Gothic Philtower (1927).

"Okie Deco" (so named by proud Tulsa locals) was always accepted as a popular middle-class expression of modernism that was meant to appeal to everyone. Certainly the rugged oil millionaires themselves projected and supported this sensibility. Streamlined Deco roadside strip architecture in the Greater Tulsa area included Texaco service stations designed by Walter Dorwin Teague, a chain of Silver Castle fast-food restaurants, supermarkets, and auto showrooms. Curvilinear and angular molded-concrete mixed easily with glass brick, aluminum, neon, tile, and baked glass-enamel on metal to create the overall effect of streamlining on a new or old building in the 1930s. Unfortunately, many of the smaller, nonelitist streamlined or populist Deco buildings have disappeared from the roadside landscape altogether, and fewer and fewer examples can be studied today except in documented photographs.

In singling out the Okie Deco of Tulsa to stand next to the Skyscraper Deco of New York City, one should not forget the Pueblo Deco of Albuquerque, New Mexico, with its Navaho imagery—canoes, skulls, swastika zigzags, ceremonial masks, war shields, drums, and longhorn skulls—much of it done in terra-cotta friezes or in tile work. Downtown Albuquerque's Kimo Theater (restored in 1982) is a prime example of Pueblo Deco.

Other cities to visit in search of Deco architectural details would certainly include Chicago and Kansas City, Missouri, and, of course, Los Angeles, San Francisco, and Oakland. As a matter of fact, all major cities have prominent Art Deco structures such as

Terra-cotta detail of Grecian-style Art Deco nude with cornucopia of fruit, on Warehouse Market Building, Tulsa, Oklahoma.

office towers, movie theaters, auto showrooms, railroad and bus stations, warehouses, high schools, and administration buildings. Certain popular architectural oddities or twentieth-century wonders like diners, gas stations, bowling alleys, early chain restaurants, modernistic private homes, and suburban Art Deco apartment buildings can be found almost anywhere. A reawakened interest in Art Deco is occurring in such diverse cities and towns as Corpus Christi, Dallas and Fort Worth (where the style is known as Cowtown Deco and Cowtown Moderne), Spokane (where a 1930s moderne Montgomery Ward warehouse was recently converted into the new City Hall), Seattle, Racine, Madison, St. Paul, Minneapolis, Charleston, Butte, Honolulu, Fairbanks, and even in Oregon's forests in connection with the WPA-built lodges of the National Park system. Preservation groups in these places are discovering, documenting, and watching over important landmarks of the 1920s and '30s that might otherwise be demolished by the wrecker's ball.

DOLORES DEL RIO

A visit to Hollywood's most amazing home, where dwell Cedric Gibbons, the artist, and Dolores Del Rio, his famed screen star wife

PHOTOGRAPHY BY HURRELL.

The home of Dolores Del Rio and Cedric Gibbons, modernistic in the extreme, is recognized as a forerunner in a severely simple style of architecture that is rapidly becoming popular

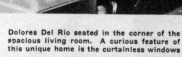

Dolores Del Rio seated in the corner of the spacious living room. A curious feature of this unique home is the curtainless windows

Dolores and Cedric in the library, a paradise of comfort for tired nerves—embellished by hundreds of books within easy reach of a luxurious lounge

Dolores and Cedric Gibbons before the fireplace in the living room. Here they often give very delightful parties

Dolores del Rio and Cedric Gibbons in their modernistic home, Hollywood *magazine, August 1931.*

Dolores Del Rio Goes Moderne

In the early 1930s very few could afford to own a modernistic home such as the "House of Tomorrow" designed by architect George Fred Keck for Chicago's Century of Progress Exposition of 1933–34. Usually such a home was like a futuristic dream that seemed far, far off to American families struggling through the Great Depression; they had to be content to experience modernism either in the movies or when visiting the palatial Radio City Music Hall in Rockefeller Center or, perhaps, their own downtown bank, office building, or remodeled drugstore or beauty parlor. It seemed only the truly elite or those who enjoyed a theatrical life could "go Moderne" in those bleak days. However, glamorous movie stars have always been exceptions to the rule; although those who land on top in the film industry have always had their ups and downs, most could afford to act according to whim, randomly changing the architecture of their life-style when they were so moved.

Hollywood magazine of August 1931 featured an article entitled "Dolores del Rio Goes Moderne" by Harry D. Wilson, who described del Rio's changeover from the El Rancho Mexicana look to that of an ultra–Art Moderne Vamp after she married M-G-M art director Cedric Gibbons. Gibbons developed into the leading exponent in Hollywood for Art Deco or Moderne movie sets following his return from the Paris exposi-

Sally Blane in A Dangerous Affair.

Gloria Stuart in Old Dark House.

Betty Grable, Paramount player in Campus Dormitory, modeling a Deco-style black-brimmed felt hat with a high-draped crown of pink wool crepe. And in a Paramount publicity still, 1939.

tion of 1925. In the fan-magazine story, Senorita del Rio asserted, "I am aching to play the sophisticated roles of modern drama after having been French, Russian, Indian, Gypsy, Spanish—everything in fact, but a Modern!"

Her chance to be "Moderne" came in 1933 in *Flying Down to Rio* with Gene Raymond, Fred Astaire, and Ginger Rogers. Unfortunately, though her looks were praised (she was often described as the most beautiful woman in the world), her acting rarely received good notices. She eventually divorced the husband who orchestrated her changeover, but not before posing for photographers in her new Hollywood Moderne house, which in status, was a step above her former Spanish Adobe Hacienda.

Left: Lillian Harvey in a sleek Deco setting from My Weakness.

Miami Moderne

The Miami Design Preservation League was formed in 1976 by the enterprising and dedicated team of Barbara Baer Capitman and Leonard Horowitz. In May 1979, the National Register of Historic Places conferred historic status on the one-mile-square Miami Beach Art Deco District, the first such designation for an area comprising buildings then less than fifty years old. Old Miami Beach's many low-rise moderne hotels, apartment buildings, commercial storefronts, public buildings, and theaters were all constructed between 1935 and 1945 by a handful of European-born New York architects influenced by the Buck Rogers–Futuristic Moderne style they saw at the 1933–34 Chicago Century of Progress Exposition. These men were also inspired by advanced architectural renderings for the ultramodern buildings planned as early as 1935 for the New York World's Fair of 1939–40.

The clean, sweeping, aerodynamic, streamlined speed forms of the South Miami Beach buildings —the curvilinear juxtaposed against stark angles—with stepped-up protruding towers and cantilevered window shades, fall into the more specific categories of both Depression Moderne and Streamline Moderne. Since the term Art Deco is now widely used as the umbrella for many interrelated modernistic styles of the 1920s and '30s, it has become the term mainly associated with the Miami Beach Historic District.

"The Orange Blossom Special," all-Pullman luxury train, "The deluxe winter season favorite between New York and Florida resorts followed the route of the Silver Meteor and the Silver Star, leader of Seaboard's popular 'Silver Fleet.'" Colortone linen postcard, 1940.

A corporate king reads Fortune magazine with his wire-haired terrier in elegant Florida setting. Fortune, December 1932.

While it is true that many of Miami's buildings have fun-Deco ornamentation on their exteriors and interiors, the main thrust and breathtaking impact of the district is decidedly Moderne with a strong Bauhaus influence. In visiting Miami Beach, it is as if one were transported back in time to a futuristic city within a city similar to those imagined at a 1930s world's fair. These visionary fairs also applied Deco ornamentation to streamlined pavilions and used murals and bas-reliefs as architectural detail.

Art Deco architecture made its first appearance in Miami in 1929 when the fluted geometric Sears, Roebuck Tower shot up into the sky, while new modern-

style buildings were added to commercial developments along Biscayne Boulevard. The Mahi-Shrine Temple (now the Biscayne Boulevard shopping arcade), built in 1930 by Robert Law Weed, is a classic example of the stepped-back facade of the Art Deco style, with turrets, multifaceted planes, and imposing sculptured figurines of Seminole Indians placed in the building's upper corners. The Bass Museum of Art, formerly the Miami Beach Public Library, also erected in 1930, was designed by Russel T. Pancoast. This Mayan-like structure is faced in "keystone," a type of coral rock indigenous to the Florida Keys. An Art Deco bas-relief on this building oddly features Christopher Columbus's three ancient sailing vessels with China Clipper flying boats soaring above. Would that Columbus had had a Clipper at his disposal in 1492.

The Miami Beach hotels and apartment buildings, constructed following the hurricane of 1926 and throughout the 1930s and early '40s, were meant to boost the Depression-weary economy in that city by creating a

The Park Central Hotel at 630 Ocean Drive, Miami Beach, Florida, was built in 1937 by architect Henry Hohauser; it was redeveloped in the 1980s by Tony Goldman.

Promotional booklet for the Miami Beach Art Deco District, published by the Miami Design Preservation League, Barbara Baer Capitman, editor, collage cover illustration by Sandra Werner, 1980.

Opposite: Flamingo lithograph-on-metal table coaster. Change trays and serving trays are to be found in this same pink, green, and black tropical design.

new tropical vacation area that would draw tourists and permanent residents to a "progressive" Florida. The 1920s Spanish Mission or Mediterranean style of Coral Gables and Palm Beach seemed too grandiose for Miami Beach, which wanted to attract more diversified middle-class vacationers to its balmy shores.

Today many of the Deco buildings have been painted in pastel hues of azure blue to match the color of the ocean, and this is playfully mixed and matched with seashell pink, rose, lime green, turquoise, or aquamarine. All white stucco or ferro-concrete buildings are often trimmed in these colors or in earth brown, sand sepia, sunflower yellow, or gladiola red. The new intense, nurserylike pastels on buildings give off the

Mark and Eric's Variety Store, featuring discount groceries and sundries, in the Art Deco district at 6th and Washington streets, Miami Beach, Florida. This colorful mauve pink and aqua facade was painted by the architect Leonard Horowitz who in the 1980s orchestrated much of the pastel coloring for the Art Deco buildings in Miami Beach.

Friedman's Bakery at Washington and 7th, Miami Beach, Florida.

overall impression of an array of giant wedding or birthday cakes. In keeping with the streamlined shapes of most of Miami Beach's buildings, which sometimes seem to resemble luxury ocean liners floating on sand, rows of porthole windows, glass bricks, and painted "racing-stripe" lines were added as decorative accents. Sundecks, pipe railings, and repetitive wave effects add to the nautical feeling inherent in these unique, showy modern structures. Bas-relief panels, applied plaster wall sculpture, painted murals, decorative tiles, and etched glass feature tropical seascapes like moonlit beaches with palm trees, WPA workers, state historical themes, pink flamingos, white whooping cranes, pelicans standing in a punk grass swamp, bloated fish, leaping porpoises or swordfish,

seahorses, dolphins, seashells, mythic sea gods like Neptune, mermaids, fauna, flora, sunbursts, tiered fountains, and sailboats. These Florida Deco images, which had great popularity in the mid- to late 1930s, '40s, and '50s all over America, may also be found as building decor at northeastern seacoast beach resorts like Asbury Park, Spring Lake, and Atlantic City in New Jersey or Jones Beach and Rye Beach, both in New York.

Ziggurats and vertical, floating, and spiked trylons appear on Miami Beach buildings with towers, but most often house and hotel rooftops are flat. Occasionally a bright tiled roof has been added to a moderne structure, borrowed from the Spanish Mediterranean style of the 1920s. Miami Beach hotels and

Six postcards of Art Moderne–style 1930s hotels (left to right): Corsair Hotel, Leslie Hotel, Olympic Hotel, Simone Hotel, Greystone Hotel, Otis Hotel and Villas. Original Miami Beach Colortone hotel series.

CORSAIR HOTEL
Directly on the Ocean
MIAMI BEACH, FLORIDA

LESLIE HOTEL
Overlooking Beautiful Park and Ocean
MIAMI BEACH, FLORIDA

Hotel
Olympic
456 Ocean Drive
MIAMI BEACH, FLORIDA

SIMONE HOTEL.   321 OCEAN DRIVE, MIAMI BEACH, FLA.

ON OCEAN FRONT WITH PRIVATE BEACH

GREYSTONE HOTEL
MIAMI BEACH, FLORIDA

THE OTIS   ON THE OCEAN AT 93RD   MIAMI BEACH

Miami Beach, where Cuban rice, bean, and flan restaurants coexist alongside kosher delicatessens. Fresh fruit, particularly oranges and grapefruit, and strong Cuban coffees are available in small retail establishments on every block.

To get a feeling of what a romantic place Miami Beach must have been in 1941, one need only view the Betty Grable 20th Century-Fox movie *Moon over Miami*, with Robert Cummings, Carole Landis, Charlotte Greenwood, and Jack Haley. Dancing in a moderne nightclub to the title tune, Betty and co-star Don Ameche made the point that Miami Beach in technicolor was a glamorous place for a vacation.

Restored Miami Beach hotels like the splendid

The Cardozo Hotel, 1300 Ocean Drive, poster design by Woody Vondracek for Art Deco Hotels, 1980s.

The Victor Hotel, 1144 Ocean Drive, poster by Woody Vondracek.

apartment complexes were lit up with flowing, colorful neon for both decor and for large hotel-apartment signs, which were often in Deco-style lettering with aluminum casing housing the neon tubing.

Splendid Deco-Moderne interiors included building materials of chrome and frosted glass for wall sconces, elaborate chandeliers, colorful geometric terrazzo floors, Vitrolite and marble trim, and bronze, chromium, nickel, stainless steel, and Monel metal for railings and grillwork. Modernistic chairs designed by Alvar Aalto and Russel Wright can still be spotted in hotel and apartment-building lobbies or lined up on spacious, open porches.

A heavy Caribbean atmosphere exists throughout

Miami wear, men's lightweight suits from Howard Clothes, Spring-Summer Tropical Collection, 1937.

Carlyle, Waldorf, and Cardozo with their exquisite Art Deco cafés and cocktail lounges and elegant lobbies, now attract guests in search of a truly Tropical Deco experience.

A walking tour of Old Miami Beach's Art Deco District should include the Cardozo, 1300 Ocean Drive, designed in 1939 by Henry Hohauser and restored as a demonstration project by Art Deco Hotels in 1979; the Carlyle, 1250 Ocean Drive, designed by Kiehnel & Elliot in 1941; the Plymouth Hotel, 2035 Park Avenue, designed by Anton Skislewicz in 1940 and based on the Trylon from the 1939 New York World's Fair; the Waldorf Towers, 860 Ocean Drive, designed by Albert Anis in 1937; the Breakwater, 940 Ocean Drive, designed by Anton Skislewicz in 1939; the Victor, 1144 Ocean Drive, designed by L. Murray Dixon in 1937 and featuring a beautiful flamingo mural in the lobby and Deco-patterned terrazzo floors; the Palmer House, 119 Collins Avenue, designed by L. Murray Dixon in 1939; and the Primrose Hotel, 1120 Collins Avenue, designed by V. H. Nellenbogen in 1935, featuring etched-glass windows with flamingos, fish, and palm trees. You will see many more fabulous hotels along Ocean Drive between 5th and 15th streets.

The tall skyscraper hotels with fantastic Deco towers include the National at 1677 Collins Avenue, the Delano at 1685 Collins Avenue, and the Ritz Plaza at 1701 Collins Avenue. Lincoln Road, the "Fifth Avenue of the South," was one of the first shopping areas in the country to close its main street for shoppers and strollers (in 1960). The recently restored Española Way, used as a typical "Latin" street in movies and on television's "Miami Vice," is the location of two of Miami Beach's early hotels, the Clay and the Cameo, both built in 1925 by Robert A. Taylor. Washington Avenue is the main commercial strip, with bakeries, variety stores, restaurants, theaters, the dazzling Post Office Building (at Washington and 12th Street), and other unique Deco/Moderne structures.

The success of the Miami Design Preservation League has influenced organizations in other cities with important Art Deco edifices to follow in its path to preservation and restoration, including Tulsa's Junior League and societies in Kansas City, Baltimore, Philadelphia, Washington, and elsewhere. Organizations like the Society for Commercial Archaeology are also instrumental in preservation activities for Art Deco buildings. In Miami Beach, "signature" in the National Register gives owners incentives to maintain and preserve property through tax advantages, but it does not always protect historic buildings from greedy speculators and developers who want to tear them down and erect high-rise condos for quick profit. The New Yorker on Collins Avenue was wrecked even after the area was declared historic, despite vehement protests from concerned citizenry.

The "Moon over Miami" look: sultry movie goddess–pinup girl Betty Grable in the 1940s wearing tropical-print rayon shirt-blouse typical of what is avidly collected and reproduced today.

Florida Deco

Authentic period "Florida Deco" or "Tropical Deco" artifacts exist in the form of popular souvenir merchandise from the 1930s, '40s, and '50s—the sun-and-fun heyday of the Art Deco district. Ubiquitous flamingo crockery and glass statuary, alligator ashtrays, seashell lamps, vintage tropical-bird jewelry featuring cranes, flamingos, pelicans or gulls are also collectible, as is the occasional rare-find Hawaiian-style rayon or silk shirt or scarf with Miami Beach images on them or a man's silk tie with a jumping swordfish or a diving girl in a swimsuit and "Miami, Florida" inscribed just under the image. The Royal Haeger Pottery Company utilized panthers, leopards, tigers, cranes, and birds on its vases and TV mood lamps.

Decorative glazed-ceramic knickknack featuring a pair of Deco fish, height 6 in., 1930s.

Tropical leaf vat-dyed drapery and upholstery fabric, 1940s.

Hand-painted water pitcher featuring a stylized fish, modern streamlines, and bubbles, made in Japan, ca. 1930.

Carved ivory-colored Catalin flamingo dress pin.

Large-leaf Brazilian-style floral fabrics are another aspect of Florida Deco, and many of these designs incorporate panthers, parrots, cockatoos, and cranes into their overall patterns. This type of popular Art Deco–mode "Pink Flamingo" type merchandise is still being produced and sentimentally evokes the nostalgic imagery of sun-splashed Florida.

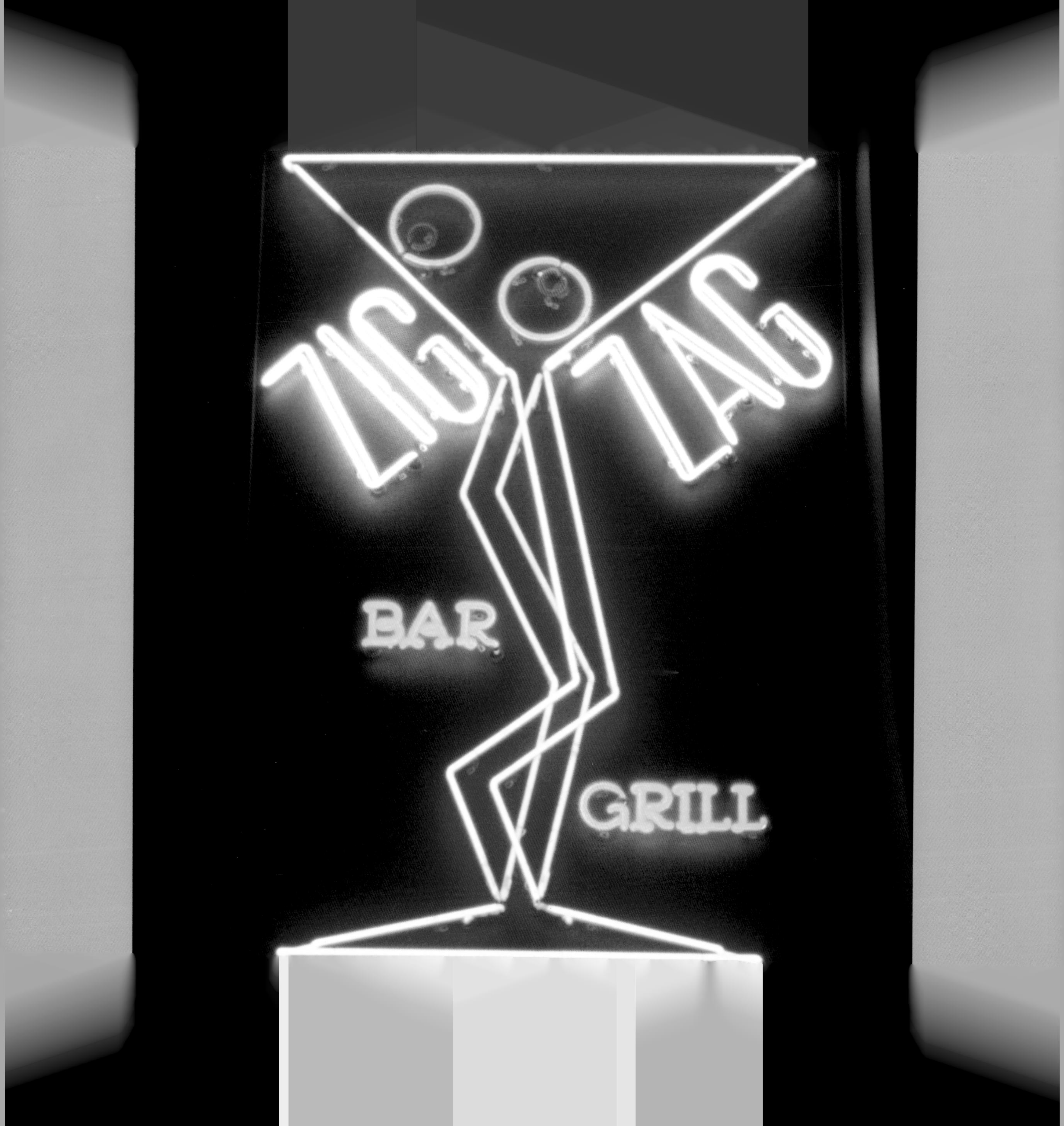
ZIG ZAG
BAR
GRILL

ECHO DECO

Echo Deco would seem like a valid term to cover the wide range of "new" Art Deco objects produced during the late 1960s, '70s, '80s, and '90s revivals as well as the reproductions copied from original 1920s and '30s period pieces. This would also include "new" Deco architecture, furniture, and interior design elements such as wallpaper, rugs, and Deco prints.

The art direction in films like the innovative *Pennies from Heaven* (1981) and Woody Allen's *Radio Days* (1987), as well as the costume and set design in Broadway musicals such as David Merrick's *Forty-Second Street* or *Oh, Kay* have contributed to the retro trend for the new-old by recreating the minute details of the Deco era. Record albums from these and other stylized nostalgia films and musicals, as well as the rereleased, vintage singer-band recordings from the 1920s, '30s, and '40s on 33⅓ or compact discs, re-pressed from original 78s, are in themselves collected by a growing number of enthusiasts of the Deco period. Large "nostalgia" bins at most record stores exist to satisfy the continuing yesteryear demand.

Sarsaparilla, a gift-novelty firm run by entrepreneur Les Sackin, reproduces Art Deco mood lamps, bookends, and decorative statuary copied directly from the original Frankart, Inc., figurines. These pieces fit easily into the new black, gray, and white high-tech Deco mode in home decor, and they are distinguishable from the original Frankarts by their use of a thicker, shinier enamel. Although they are almost identical in form, they are not stamped "Frankart," are not dated, and do not show the fine attention to detail displayed by the Arthur von Frankenburg novelty nude-nymphet forms of the 1920s and '30s. Sarsaparilla also manufactures a replica of an airplane lamp in the Industrial Moderne style in chrome and frosted glass that is difficult to tell from the original item. Ubiquitous novelty pink-flamingo ceramic statuary, vases, salt and pepper shakers, ashtrays, lamps, teapots, creamer-sugar sets, and other objects are reproduced in the thousands by Sarsaparilla and other companies.

Animated neon sign invites customers in for a martini cocktail. Located in New York on 23^d Street near the Chelsea Hotel, this bar and grill set forth a new standard for the Echo Deco design in the late 1980s.

Following the John Water's movie *Pink Flamingoes* (1973), pink trash/camp bird figurines somehow mysteriously found their way into the world of new Deco collectibles. Today new plastic bubble gum–pink flamingos produced to stick into the ground add a touch of avant-garde banality to the front lawn in the 1940s and '50s manner.

Deco-style painted-on-reverse glass stand-up frames, usually in two contrasting colors, are also being produced again for the Deco-boutique market; most have pictures of Golden Age movie stars like Garbo, Harlow, Lombard, Errol Flynn, or Clark Gable inserted in them for display purposes, just as they did when sold at dime stores in the Depression.

Fiesta-ware and Harlequin crockery, as well as transparent, colored Depression dishware, have also been reproduced for mass-marketing in department stores, gift shops, and the dime store. The Homer-Laughlin Company introduced "new" Fiesta colors in the 1980s, but they were the decorator-favored colors of white, pink, and black so as not to compete with the original 1930s and '40s Fiesta orange-red, deep blue, green, yellow, and ivory that collectors of the vintage sets admire. The new Fiesta set of cups, saucers, plates, vases, and other dinnerware pieces is heavier than the original, and the glaze is thicker. The

Painted plastic Chiparus-style Christmas tree ornaments sold at better department stores during the 1980s Christmas seasons.

Hall China Company has also reproduced their line of fanciful Moderne teapots, water jugs, and vases, and again they are easily distinguishable from the originals and usually make use of different color glazes.

The reprinting of original posters and reinterpretations of Deco graphics for posters and greeting cards by today's artisans have produced a profusion in the boutique marketplace. One can easily purchase a repro of a "Normandie" travel poster or an Erté *Vogue* cover or a Maxfield Parrish "blue" scene, but usually the age of the paper, the state-of-the-art printing processes, the missing printer's markings, and the low cost make no pretense at presenting one of these as an original run.

Likewise new plastic jewelry, bracelets, dress pins, and earrings are sometimes to be found at flea markets, garage sales, antique shows, and in shops mistakenly masquerading as "Catalin" or "Bakelite." However, these newer jewelry pieces are usually of

Deco tablet tin from the early 1970s.

lighter weight; older industrial plastics that are now highly sought after as Deco artifacts show inevitable age discoloration and are sometimes even marked "Catalin" or "Celluloid." Reputable antique-jewelry dealers usually will explain the differences to a prospective uninitiated buyer and will not handle reproduced plastic. Original Catalin jewelry parts are also reassembled by enterprising jewelry merchants to fill the ever-increasing demand. Much of the new "Echo Deco" assembly-line mass-produced boutique merchandise falls into the category of "the instant collectible," which some buyers hope will appreciate in value; for the most part, however, appreciation is far below that of the original vintage artifacts. This does not mean that it is not fun to collect and use the new

Album cover featuring a Deco room setting for the reissue of hits from the Geraldo Orchestra, the popular 1930s English dance band.

Laminated paper shopping bag from the Smithsonian Institution's "Hollywood—Legend and Reality" exhibition, with lithographed poster art by Doug Johnson, 1986.

Newly refurbished Art Deco chandeliers illuminate the main sales floor of the flagship Macy's department store on 34th Street in New York. Created for Macy's by Rambusch Co., New York.

"instants" for practical purposes, for decor, or as wearables. For instance, Stewart Richer's line of retro-clothing, sold nationwide in boutiques and department stores and at his signature store on Fifth Avenue at 14th Street in Manhattan, includes Hawaiian Deco-patterned rayon shirts, bathrobes, skirts, and bathing trunks copied from original 1930s and '40s designs. These well-made garments feature palm trees, tropical leafage, leaping fish, pineapples, hula girls, Hawaiian kings, tropical hibiscus flowers, cowboys, and other "original-style" patterns in bold, brilliant colors with authentic coconut-shell buttons added for the sake of "authenticity."

In the burgeoning field of interior and exterior restoration, where we see smart diners being returned to their original stainless steel, chrome, neon, glass-brick, and leatherette design details, new business enterprises have surfaced to accommodate the growing needs of authentic restoration. Rudi Stern, a forerunner of the new breed of neon craftsmen-entrepreneurs, manufactures fanciful and imaginative interpretations of sculptural neon, as well as artful reproductions of original neon artifacts, including octagonal neon clocks and signs with nude girls perched on the edge of cocktail glasses. From his Manhattan headquarters, Let There Be Neon, Stern also creates new neon for industrial and commercial projects and maintains and restores neon signage still extant from New York's neon heyday.

Bloomingdale's and Macy's department stores in New York City have both renovated their main floors in Deco-style decor. Bloomingdale's, decked out in flashy black glass, chrome, and gold brass, has created a new, well-lit Deco environment in which to sell its perfume and cosmetics products. Macy's had five great Deco chandeliers designed and executed by the New York City firm of Rambusch, which specializes in

authentic restoration for theaters, stores, and churches. Paul Goldberger, the architecture critic, gave a salutation to the splendid Macy's restoration in the *New York Times* (December 1, 1983): "It is expansive and gracious, with precisely the right combination of elegance and bustle that should characterize a great selling floor—an intelligent and knowing essay on the Art Deco theme."

Art Deco wall sconce designed in the 1930s by Rambusch Co., reissued for the 1990s.

The Waldorf-Astoria hotel has tastefully restored its Park Avenue Art Deco entranceway, including uncovering an array of original hand-painted Deco murals. Circling the mosaic-tiled floor of the foyer there is a balcony cocktail, coffee, and tea service lounge, and the Grand Ballroom has also been splendidly redone according to the hotel's original Art Deco style. The Rainbow Room on top of Rockefeller Center is now also a glitteringly restored Deco nightclub in keeping with the theme of the center itself.

Clearly, with all the many reproductions, reinterpretations, and restorations of this classic modern style happening everywhere, Deco is here to stay. This does not mean that all attempts at recreating an Art Deco environment or atmosphere are always authentic or gracious. Too often the wrong garish colors or overly bold design interpretations, such as those used in new hotel and motel lobbies or gambling casinos, are

Nineteen eighty-seven poster for the Zigzag Club, 206 W. 23rd Street, New York, Kenneth Kneitel design/ Doug Taylor illustration.

a harsh, makeshift jumble that is far removed from the classic, more subtle simplicity, and original intentions of Art Deco. While startling bright colors like those used in terra-cotta and mosaic tiles, terrazzo floors, and WPA murals were often used originally, they were never meant to be psychedelic, loud, or cheap.

Nevertheless, there are to be found some splendid examples of "Echo Deco."

The Deco Parade marches on!

Souvenir booklet issued in the 1980s heralding the Art Deco restoration of the Waldorf Cocktail Terrace.

Zephyr Club Chair in leather and polished chrome, newly manufactured by the Jazz Art Deco Revival Interiors, Los Angeles and New York. This type of streamlined club chair was originally produced in the 1930s by Royalchrome of Chicago, Illinois.

ART DECO SOCIETIES

American Art Deco Societies

Art Deco Society of New York
P.O. Box 160, Planetarium Station
New York, NY 10024
www.artdeco.org

Art Deco Society of Washington
P.O. Box 42722
Washington DC 20015
www.adsw.org

Art Deco Society of Boston
1 Murdock Terrace
Brighton, MA 02135

Art Deco Society of the Palm Beaches
325 SW 29th Avenue
Delray Beach, Florida 33445

Detroit Area Art Deco Society
P.O. Box 1393
Royal Oak, MI 48068
www.daads.org

Chicago Art Deco Society
P.O. Box 1116
Evanston, IL 60204
www.chicagoartdecosociety.com

Tulsa Art Deco Society
2926 East 39th Street
Tulsa, Oklahoma 74105

Art Deco Society of California
100 Bush Street, Suite 511
San Francisco, CA 94104
www.art-deco.org

Art Deco Society of Los Angeles
P.O. Box 972
Hollywood, CA 90078
www.adsla.org

Sacramento Art Deco Society
PO Box 162836
Sacramento, CA 95816
www.sacdeco.org

Art Deco Society Northwest
1216 Devon Loop NE
Olympia, WA 98506
www.art-decoNW.org

Presentation Groups

Miami Design Preservation League
P.O. Box 190180
Miami Beach, FL 33119
www.mdpl.org

Tulsa Historical Society
2445 South Peoria
Tulsa, Oklahoma 74114
www.tulsahistory.org

Friends of Terra Cotta
c/o Tunick
771 West End Ave #1DE
New York, NY 10025
www.preserve.org/fotc/fotc.htm

International Art Deco Societies

Canadian Art Deco Society
1030 – 470 Granville Street
Vancouver, BC V6 C1V5

Art Deco Society of Toronto
www.artdecotoronto.com

Art Deco Society of Montreal
www.artdecomontreal.com

The Twentieth Century Society
70 Cowcross St.
London EC1M 6EJ

Cape Art Deco
P.O. Box 101
Piketburg 7370
South Africa
www.artdeco2003.com

Durban Art Deco Society
14 Lawrence Road
Durban 4001 South Africa

Art Deco Society Inc. (Melbourne)
P.O. Box 17
Camberwell, Victoria 3124 Australia
www.artdeco.org.au

Art Deco Society of NSW
Willoughby, Australia
www.welcome.to/artdeconsw.com

The Twentieth Century Heritage Society
of New South Wales Australia
http://twentieth.org.au/

Art Deco Trust Napier (New Zealand)
www.artdeconapier.com

Art Deco Society of Auckland
P.O. Box 109-304
Auckland, New Zealand
www.artdeco.org.NZ

BIBLIOGRAPHY

Books

Albrecht, Donald. *Designing Dreams: Modern Architecture in the Movies*. New York: Harper & Row and Museum of Modern Art, 1986.

Arwas, Victor. *Art Deco*. New York: Harry N. Abrams, 1980.

Battersby, Martin. *The Decorative Twenties*. New York: Walker & Co., 1969.

_____ . *The Decorative Thirties*. New York: Walker & Co., 1971.

Bayley, Stephen. *In Good Shape: Style in Industrial Products, 1900–1960*. New York: Van Nostrand Reinhold, 1979.

Berkow, Nancy. *Fiesta*. Radner, PA: Wallace Homestead, 1978.

Bletter, Rosemarie Haag, and Cervin Robinson. *Skyscraper Style: Art Deco New York*. New York: Oxford University Press, 1975.

Breeze, Carla. *American Art Deco- Regional Differences of Deco Architecture Across America*. New York: Thames and Hudson, 2003

_____ . *Pueblo Deco*. New York: Rizzoli, 1990

Bush, Donald J. *The Streamlined Decade*. New York: George Braziller, 1975.

Capitman, Barbara Baer. *Deco Delights*. New York: E. P. Dutton, 1988

Cerwinske, Laura. *Tropical Deco: The Architecture and Design of Old Miami Beach*. New York: Rizzoli, 1981.

Chipman, Jack, and Judy Stangler,. *Bauer Pottery*. Culver City, CA: California Spectrum, 1982.

Cohen, Judith Singer. *Cowtown Moderne: Art Deco Architecture of Fort Worth, Texas*. College Station, TX: Texas A & M University Press, 1988

DiNoto, Andrea. *Art Plastic: Designed for Living*. New York: Abbeville Press, 1984.

Dreyfuss, Henry. *A Record of Industrial Designs, 1929–1946*. New York: Davis, Delaney, 1946.

Duncan, Alastair. *American Art Deco*. New York: Harry N. Abrams, 1986.

Friedman, Marilyn. *Selling Good Design*. New York: Rizzolli Publishers, 2003.

Fusco, Tony. *The Instant Expert: Art Deco*. New York: House of Collectibles, 2004.

_____ . *The Official Identification and Price Guide to Art Deco*. New York: House of Collectibles, 1988.

Gold-Levi, Vicki and Steven Heller. *Cuba Style*. New York: Harry N. Abrams, 2000

Goldfarb, Alice. *Hopes and Ashes: The Birth of Modern Times*. New York: Free Press, 1986.

Grief, Martin. *Depression Modern: The Thirties Style in America*. New York: Universe Books, 1975.

Harrison, Helen. *Dawn of a New Day: The New World's Fair, 1939–40*. New York: Queens Museum and New York University Press, 1980.

Hennessey, William J. *Russel Wright: American Designer*. Cambridge: M.I.T. Press, 1985.

Hiller, Bevis. *Art Deco*. New York: E. P. Dutton, 1968.

_____ . *The World of Art Deco*. Minneapolis: Minneapolis Institute of Arts and New York: E. P. Dutton, 1971.

Hine, Thomas. *Popluxe*. New York: Alfred A. Knopf, 1986.

Hirshorn, Paul, and Steven Izenour. *White Towers*. Cambridge: M.I.T. Press, 1979.

Hooper, Rodney. *Modern Furniture Making and Design*. Peoria, IL: Manual Arts Press, 1939.

James, Theodore. *The Empire State Building*. New York: Harper & Row, 1975.

Jenkins, Alan. *The Twenties*. New York: Universe Books, 1974.

_____ .*The Thirties*. New York: Stein & Day, 1976.

Johnson, Stuart. *American Modern, 1925–1940*. New York: Harry N. Abrams, 2000.

Katz, Sylvia. *Plastics: Common Objects, Classic Designs*. New York: Harry N. Abrams, 1984.

Kery, Patricia Frantz. *Art Deco Graphics*. New York: Harry N. Abrams, 1986.

Kimura, Katsu. *Art Deco Package Collection*. Japan: Rikuyo-Sha, 1985.

Klein, Dan, and Nancy A. McClelland. *In the Deco Style*. New York: Rizzoli, 1986.

Langdon, Philip. *Orange Roofs, Golden Arches: The Architecture of American Chain Restaurants*. New York: Alfred A. Knopf, 1986.

Loewy, Raymond. *Industrial Design*. Winchester, MA: Faber & Faber, 1979.

Mandelbaum, Howard and Eric Myers. *Screen Deco*. Santa Monica: Hennessey & Ingalls, (re-issue 2002)

McClinton, Katharine Morrison. *Art Deco: A Guide for Collectors*. New York: Clarkson N. Potter, 1972.

Meikle, Jeffrey L. Twentieth-Century Limited: *Industrial Design in America, 1925–1939*. Philadelphia: Temple University Press, 1979.

Naylor, Gillian. *The Bauhaus Reassessed*. New York: E.P. Dutton, 1985.

Phillips, Cabel. *From the Crash to the Blitz, 1929–1939*. New York: Macmillan, 1969.

Pildas, Ave. *Art Deco Los Angeles*. Special photographic study. New York: Harper & Row, 1977.

Pilgrim, Dianne H., Dickran Tashjian and Richard Guy Wilson. *The Machine Age in America, 1918–1941*. New York: Brooklyn Museum and Harry N. Abrams, 1986.

Pulos, Arthur V., *American Design Ethos: A History of Industrial Design*. Cambridge: M.I.T. Press, 1983.

Scarlett, Frank, and Marjorie Townley. *Arts Decoratifs 1925: A Personal Recollection of the Paris Exhibition*. New York: St. Martins Press, 1975.

Sembach, Klaus Jurgen. *Style 1930*. New York: Universe Books, 1971.

Sideli, John. *Classic Plastic Radios of the 1930s and 1940s*. New York: E.P. Dutton, 1990.

Stern, Bill. *California Pottery*. San Francisco: Chronicle Books, 2000

Striner, Richard, and Hans Wirz. *Washington Art Deco: Art Deco in the Nation's Capitol*. Washington, D.C.: Smithsonian Institution Press, 1984.

Terhune, Albert Payson. *Dogs*. Akron, OH and New York: Saalfield Publishing, 1940.

Van de Lemme, Arie. *A Guide to Art Deco Style*. Secaucus, NJ: Chartwell Books, 1986.

Van Doren, Harold. *Industrial Design,* New York: McGraw-Hill, 1940.

Veronesi, Giulia. *Style and Design, 1909–1929*. New York: George Braziller, 1968.
Vlack, Don. *Art Deco Architecture in New York, 1920–1940*. New York: Harper& Row, 1974.

Whitmyer, Margaret and Kenn. *The Collector's Guide to Hall China*. Paducah, KN: Collectors Books, 1986.

Wurts, Richard, et al. *The New York World's Fair, 1939–40*. New York: Dover, 1977.

Special Publications

American Union of Decorative Artists and Craftsmen. *Modern American Design*. New York: Ives Washburn, 1930.

Benton, Charlotte, Tim Benton, and Jhislaine Wood. *Art Deco, 1910-1939*. New York: Bulfinch Press with the Victoria and Albert Museum, London, 2003.

Art Deco Society of New York. *Art Deco Newsletter.* vols. 1981-87. Ed. Glenn Loney. New York: Art Deco Society of New York, 1981-87.

Building the World of Tomorrow: Official Guide Book of the New York Word's Fair, 1939. New York: Exposition Publications, 1939.

Cohen, Daniel. "Put Your Nickel in the Slot." *Smithsonian* 16, no. 10 (January 1986): 50-61.

Fiesta. Newell, WV.: Homer Laughlin China Co., 1941.

Frankenburg, Arthur von. Catalogs for Frankart, Manufacturers of Objects of Art in Metal. New York, 1920s – 1930s.

Josen, Bob and Harriett Selzer. *Things Deco*. www.deco-echoes.com/td/

Metropolitan Dade County Office of Community and Economic Development, Historic Preservation Division. *From Wilderness to Metropolis: The History of Dade County, Florida, 1825-1940*. Dade County, FL.: MDCOCED, 1982.

Siegel, Alan A., *Smile: A Picture History of Olympic Park, 1887-1965*. 1983.

Streamlining America. Dearborn, MI: Henry Ford Museum and Greenfield Village, 1986.

Tulsa Art Deco: An Architectural Era, 1925-1942. Tulsa, Okla.: Junior League of Tulsa, 1980.

Tunick, Susan. "Architectural Terra Cotta: Its Impact on New York." *Sites* 18 (1986): 4-37.

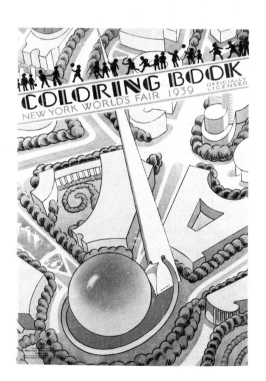

Other books by Robert Heide and John Gilman

Mickey Mouse: The Evolution, The Legend, The PHENOMENON!
Disneyana: Classic Collectibles 1925–1955
The Mickey Mouse Watch – From the Beginning of Time
New Jersey: Art of the State
O' New Jersey
Greenwich Village: A Primo Guide to True Bohemia
Home Front America: Popular Culture of the World War II Era
Box-Office Buckaroos: The Cowboy Hero From the Wild West Show to the Silver Screen
Starstruck: The Wonderful World of Movie Memorabilia
Cartoon Collectibles: 50 Years of Dime Store Memorabilia
Cowboy Collectibles
Dime-Store Dream Parade: Popular Culture 1925–1955